Mr John M. Templeton, founder of the Templeton Prize.

The Templeton Foundation Prize for Progress in Religion

By

WILBERT FORKER

WINCHESTER PRESS

Published by Winchester Press
Box 563, Howell, New Jersey 07731 USA

Library of Congress Cataloging in Publication Data

Forker, Wilbert, 1935 —
   The Templeton Foundation Prize for progress in religion.

   Originally published by Christian Journals (Ireland), Belfast.
   Includes bibliographies.
   1. Templeton Foundation — History.   2. Religion — Awards.
3. Templeton, John, 1912 —   I. Title.

BL11.A2T4534   1980   291'.079   80-17533

ISBN 0-936242-00-0

Printed in England.

CONTENTS

This is not intended to be a comprehensive history of the Templeton
Foundation Programme of Prizes but rather a journal of record
that will one day form the basis for an in-depth history.
Being a journal of record it draws on a number of sources thus
presenting much detail in its original form.
April 1977

chapter one

THE BEGINNINGS

Just what happened to the role of religion in the world? Why was there such a dichotomy between religion and science; between religion and mankind? Just why did religion no longer provide guidance for man especially as society became so topsy turvy when changes in direction were being taken without much reflection by most of mankind?

It was thoughts like these that continually concerned the mind of John Templeton. He saw the need for reflection; for in-depth study in religion as he saw the need for continued research in his own field as a financial analyst. For without this reflection and research little could happen in the whole world of investing. Yet he continually asked himself why was the Church at large, as far as the Christian faith is concerned, indeed the centres of learning of the world's religions, not undertaking more research in order that mankind may benefit from wider and deeper understanding of God and love of God.

He saw in the Nobel Prizes for Peace, Literature, Medicine and the sciences that recognition could be given to an outstanding person or group of people whose life's work brought hope for the sick, enlightenment for the intellect and the prospect of peace. Why could progress in religion not be recognized as more important than progress in all other areas combined?

For almost twenty years John Templeton reflected on this question and sought advice from a wide variety of people. Originally it was his intention to have an award for religion, similar to the Nobel Prize, in his will, but as he continued to witness the twists and turns of the 'sixties he decided to establish it during his lifetime.

When meditating and praying about the award he thought it should be for progress in Christianity. Then a number of Christian leaders advised him to design an award so that worshippers of all faiths could feel personal participation.

In asking himself who will benefit from the award John Templeton wrote: 'it would be easy indeed for the Templeton Foundation to mail a cheque for £34,000 to a world religious project each year. A different method has been chosen in the hope of vastly greater benefits.' The award is intended 'to call attention to a variety of persons who have found new ways to increase man's love of God or understanding of God.'

The turmoil of the university campus in the 'sixties turned his mind towards young people and it is his desire that those who receive the award will 'inspire more young people to devote their lives to being useful channels through which His love can flow.' He 'hopes that young people in each nation will come to regard religious careers as more exciting, dynamic and varied.'

The results of detailed research work in industry have meant much to John Templeton over the years. Working as a Certified Financial Analyst, he has seen how companies with a research programme have been able to prosper and benefit the community. He was also very conscious of the development, due to research, in the natural sciences. He was and still is somewhat disappointed at the lack of research in the field of religion. While various efforts have

2

and are being made, overall there is not much being undertaken.

This is an award for progress. It is not an award for saintliness or mere good works. It is for achieving, for pioneering a breakthrough in religious thought and understanding. It is an attempt to focus attention on those whose projects and thoughts are not yet widely known. Those who have received the award thus far are creative pacesetters in religion, who have and are helping the religious community to come to grips with a new awareness of God and so open up an era of religious thought to a wider vision of God's infinity.

Mother Teresa has displayed a new dimension to the words 'Love', 'Compassion' and 'Creating' by her devotion to the dying, the poor and the lonely.

By originating and serving as the guiding spirit of the Taizé Community, no one has done more than Roger Schutz to revitalize religion among young people of Europe.

Dr Sarvepalli Radhakrishnan, the renowned Spalding Professor of Eastern Religion and Ethics at Oxford, helped Westerners to benefit from the rich and varied insights of Eastern religions and Easterners to understand that we are all worshipping the same universal creator of us all.

And Cardinal Suenens of Belgium has made an inspiring contribution by his book *A New Pentecost* and as interpreter of the thousands of new Charismatic groups to traditional theologians. His original contributions to the reforming of the Church's structures and the prominence of the ministry of the laity have led to renewed hope and faith for many.

These recipients are helping mankind to find again an oasis of spiritual perfection and human sympathy. Progress in science we are all aware of. The exploration of outer space, man taking his first halting steps on the moon, the great breakthroughs in medicine to alleviate pain and suffering, the everyday miracles of television and common electricity are now all taken for granted.

3

But progress in religion is not so apparent, and it must be if we as the people of God are to undo the programme of destruction our flimsy and inconstant world seems to have embarked upon.

In the brochure setting out the purpose and objectives of the award the Trustees of the Foundation said: 'Progress is needed in religion as in all other dimensions of human experience and endeavour. There has been a long departure, at least in western culture, from the last synthesis when religious knowledge and scientific knowledge were organically related. It is imperative that progress in religion be accelerated as progress in other disciplines takes place.' Since the astronauts gave us those first pictures of themselves walking on the moon there has been a wider understanding of the universe. As a result a number of men argue that this demands a deeper awareness of the dimension of the spirit and of the spiritual resources available to man. The immensity of God is being made clear to many and it is this mankind should be made aware of.

Prince Philip when presenting the first award to Mother Teresa in London's historic Guildhall said: 'At first sight the idea that a prize might be able to do something for religion seems faintly absurd. . . . I respected the intention of his imaginative proposal and I have every confidence in the judges, but I doubted whether it would work. . . . but it is really Mother Teresa who has made this Prize work in the way it was intended.'

In relation to the Christian faith it was Luther who reawakened decadent Europe to the meaning of faith; it was Calvin who helped the people of Geneva to understand the sovereignty of God; it was Wesley who inspired many with the assurances that God was available to them. Such can now be seen as marked progress but it was not readily accepted as such at the time. In more recent times the French philosopher scientist and priest, Teilhard de Chardin, attempted to help his people in similar pioneering exercises but he was all but snuffed out. It is only now that the world is taking notice of the significance of the things Teilhard said.

We could get the valid impression that the leadership in the Christian church at least seems to be against that which it does not understand. Some of the great reformers have been victims of this attitude of mind. But it was their pioneering breakthroughs which set them apart as religious pacesetters of the day.

The paradox is that if there was a co-ordinated research programme in theology—in its widest sense—there would be less need for the 'closed-mind attitude'.

Another aspect that John Templeton had in mind was the role of the scientist in making God more widely known to mankind. The recent developments in the natural and life sciences have brought about a clearer understanding of the meaning of God as creator. Indeed a number of critical ethical issues, stimulated by scientific and technological developments, have forced their way into public attention. But once one starts that agonizing process of reflecting on the issues anew, much deeper issues become apparent. While for many the depths of what are called timeless issues are all too familiar the context in which they arise is new. It is this important factor John Templeton saw as crucial to an understanding of the love of God in today's world. Templeton was aware that from the life sciences the test-tube baby is estimated to be a common birth in the 'eighties. He was also aware that geneticists were on the verge of re-arranging genes and chromosomes and thereby paving the way for creating a superhuman being. With this awareness he asked himself what is the distinctive guideline the religions of the world can give to those involved in this miracle of creation showing us a part of God unheard of twenty years ago and helping us to grow again and to explore even further.

One could catalogue similar issues that today are calling for individual attention to ascertain God at work in the world.

Mr Templeton realized this new dimension to the contemporary encounter between science and theology and that some fresh thinking on the old theoretical questions like the nature of God and His relationship to the universe is now taking place. He was also concerned that teachers of the world's religions should therefore state their view of the Divine in such a way that there can be no misunderstanding of the responsibility of man for the nature of his society. Man remains finite. He is not the Lord of history, but he faces real alternatives that can lead to life or death. In such a position he needs clarity of though on issues that often seem to belong to the realm of metaphysics.

From the beginning John Templeton emphasized that in no way was he seeking to encourage syncretism. This allayed the fears if not the suspicions of a number of people who were not confined to any one particular faith. In a pointed statement he said: 'the Foundation would seek rather to focus attention on the wide variety of highlights in present-day religious thought and work. We seek not a unity of denominations or a united world religion; but rather we seek to encourage understanding of the benefits of diversity.'

So with this as our task the stage was set but much detailed planning was still necessary to ensure a credible reception for an idea that was being offered with very deep conviction and insight. An important benefit from the programme is to inspire millions of people in all religions by calling attention to the work of each recipient; but this benefit could result from extensive coverage by mass media.

Newspaper, radio and television are normally cynical and particularly of anything religious. A number give local and national coverage to items of news affecting the community as such but when it comes to innovation, initiative or indeed something like the Templeton Prize embracing the religions of the world there are indeed many questions. These questions, however, tend not to focus on the content but rather on curiosity and at times lack of knowledge of the subject.

With this in mind one had to be very careful how the media would be approached and the idea delivered in terms that would not only catch the reporter's imagination but that of the editor.

It was with some trepidation that I undertook this task of communicating to the world at large. I saw it as a challenge yet with some uncertainty on the possibility of being able to bring it off. Indeed the old cliché of: 'miracles we can perform, the impossible takes a little longer' tended to lurk at the back of my mind. The Associated Press — the international news agency with headquarters in New York — got the idea and translated it in terms of 'a Nobel Prize in Religion' — an attempt to do in and for religion what those great prizes have done for the sciences and culture. But the British press was cool, very cool. The London *Times* devoted a few paragraphs, the conservative *Daily Telegraph* a couple, the mass-circulation newspapers like the *Mirror* and *Daily Express* gave no mention and the BBC carried it only on a religious round-up bulletin of news. However, the religious newspapers gave us very good news coverage, which was sympathetic and understanding.

This first reaction presented the strategy for future relations with the media. Each year the reception has been much better and the coverage much wider than the year before. This was seen in full-page stories in *Time* magazine and *People* in the United States, front-page news headline stories in British religious papers, and photo coverage by *Paris Match* and other European periodicals, not to mention exclusive coverage in national and provincial newspapers in Asia and Australasia.

Perhaps the most evident of developments was the proposal by the BBC television to present a half-hour documentary on the Prize and the recipient each year, which in turn will be marketed to television stations around the world.

Another aspect of the organization that required much

reflection and consultation was the putting together of a panel of judges who would select the recipient each year.

Using my years as a religious correspondent and my work with the World Council of Churches it was comparatively easy to get in touch with those responsible in the major world religions to ascertain their views and opinions.

It was after such a consultation that a simple and efficient organization began to take shape.

The first panel of judges was:

The Reverend Dr Eugene Carson Blake, then General Secretary of the World Council of Churches (Presbyterian);

Professor Suniti Kumar Chatterji, National Professor of India in the Humanities (Hindu);

Sir Muhammad Zafrulla Khan, then President of the International Court of Justice in the Hague (Muslim);

Dr Margaretha Klompé, a former Minister of Cultural Affairs in the Dutch Government (Roman Catholic);

The Reverend Dr James McCord, President of Princeton Theological Seminary, New Jersey (Presbyterian);

Sir Alan Mocatta, a judge of the High Court in England (Jewish);

The Lord Abbot Kosho Ohtani, Chief Monk of the Nishi Hongwanji Temple, Japan (Buddhist);

Lord Thurlow, a former Governor of the Bahamas (Anglican);

The Right Reverend R. W. Woods, Bishop of Worcester (Anglican).

Another aspect, and an important one too, in setting up the basic organization was to choose a centre for the Prize. A number of possibilities were considered and finally reduced to two: one was to hold the presentation in a different country each year and the other to have it in one place at least initially. New York, Washington D.C., Toronto, Brussels, Geneva, Rome, London, Stuttgart, Tokyo

8

were all possible venues, but finally, because the founder of the Templeton Foundation is a British subject, London was chosen, first as a venue to inaugurate the Prize and then for the presentation each year.

It was at this stage that the connexion with St Bride's Church in Fleet Street arose. Not only is it the parish church at the centre of the British newspaper industry and on the doorsteps of the offices of the big national dailies, the wire services, radio and television, its history has been one of communicating to the world at large the message of God in the hope that mankind would respond.

There are places where history passes by with a step as light as gossamer, leaving no trace. St Bride's, 'the cathedral of Fleet Street', is not one of them. This site spans two thousand years' development of an island people. Little of importance that has happened in England's story has not been echoed in St Bride's. From the time when the Romans built here through the rise and fall of its seven previous churches, this place has been nationally, and indeed, internationally, involved. Celts, Romans, Angles, Saxons, Normans, so many people, made this place. Today, in the exchange of news, it is parish pump to the whole world.

The people who worship in this church have felt the impact of the struggle between the ancient Celtic church and the Roman Catholic Church as it grew from Augustine's impetus. In those days, too, they grappled with the alarums of theological ferment. This church has been the symbol that the Church moves on a pilgrimage of new discoveries about God. Time and the affairs of men have given to St Bride's a unique setting. The one continuing feature which has endured through all the changes is the worship of God, the worship that remains incomplete until it finds universal fellowship.

It was in this setting on 8th May, 1972, that the Templeton Prize was inaugurated with Lord Thurlow in the chair and some fifty journalists representing important radio and television stations, newspapers and magazines. With Lord Thurlow were some of the eminent judges who saw in the award a challenge for mankind to recognize once again the dimension of God in the affairs of man.

Mr John Templeton in his inaugural address said that the Prize was primarily to contribute towards increasing man's knowledge and love of God and thus releasing new and creative energies into human society. The coming together of men of goodwill, Mr Templeton said, will 'we believe, lead to a dialogue between the religions of the world. From a Christian point of view this dialogue implies neither a denial of the uniqueness of Christ nor any loss of the Christian's own commitment to Christ, but rather a genuine Christian approach to others in a human, personal, spiritual and humble way. In this dialogue we hope to share our common humanity and dignity and express our common concern for our spiritual well being.

'If we can achieve this dialogue it should open the possibility of sharing in new forms of community and common service. Each of us in our own religious tradition is witnessing from the depths of our own love to the ultimate concerns that come to expression in action and word.

'We believe that mankind is one indivisible whole. This, today, calls for a more open and humble partnership between all who worship and work towards the widening of man's knowledge and love of God. This calls for a clearer acceptance of the diversity of gifts within the major religions of the world, for each knowing his own particular gifts will help bring men to the measure of the fulness of the stature of the divine.

'We are deeply indebted to our forefathers who recorded in books their spiritual discoveries and revelations. Alive today are other persons to whom God is revealing further holy truths. The Templeton Foundation wishes to be helpful in making known more widely these new breakthroughs in man's understanding of God.'

Then came the need for somewhere to hold the presentation. London offers a particularly wide variety of suitable places ranging from the ancient historical Livery Halls to the modern Queen Elizabeth Hall on the South Bank. The historic Guildhall in the City of London was granted to us by the Corporation of London and each year the ceremony in connexion with the presentation has been held there.

Finding a recipient was not an easy matter but soon a simple procedure was established. Invitations to make nominations for the Prize, guidelines to help the nominators, were sent out to a list of two thousand people, lay and cleric, culled from the main world religions and with as even a geographical basis as possible. This method, coupled with the response from the media, was encouraging.

The judges retire on a rotation system with three retiring each year. In 1974 the three judges to retire were: Dr Blake, Dr Klompé and Lord Thurlow. They were replaced by: Her Majesty Fabiola, Queen of the Belgians (Roman Catholic); The Reverend Dr Norman Vincent Peale, Minister of Marble Collegiate Church, New York City (Reformed); and Her Serene Highness Princess Poon Pismai Diskul, President of the World Fellowship of Buddhists (Buddhist). In 1975 the retiring judges were: Professor Chatterji, Sir Alan Mocatta and Lord Ohtani. The remaining judges were joined by: His All Holiness Demetrios I, the Ecumenical Patriarch of Constantinople (Greek Orthodox); His Excellency Mr Apasaheb Balasaheb Pant, then Ambassador of India to Italy (Hindu); and Mr Edmund de Rothschild, the Treasurer of the British Council of Christians and Jews (Jewish). The three judges who retired in 1976 were: Sir Zafrulla Khan, Dr McCord and the Bishop of Worcester. They were replaced by Sir Bernard Lovell, Britain's Astronomer Royal (Methodist), the Anglican Bishop of Winchester, The Right Reverend Dr John V. Taylor, and Mr Masakazu Echigo of Japan (Buddhist).

Their task has been simplified since the Prize was first

established. Today the nominations are much more detailed so it is easier to come to a conclusion.

When the various aspects of the organization are placed together it has become clear to us that with continued evaluation the more efficient the organization becomes, this in turn makes the task of the judges easier.

chapter two

JOHN TEMPLETON PLANS TO SERVE RELIGION

John Templeton spent much time at his home in Lyford Cay in the Bahamas thinking about the award. As a financial analyst the benefits of a company or a corporation to the public and to shareholders were of the utmost importance to him. In a sense he applied this line of thought to the Prize that bears his name. In a remarkably small document which he calls 'Who benefits?' he wrote: 'It would be easy indeed for the Templeton Foundation to mail a cheque for £34,000 to a worthy religious project each year. A different method has been chosen in the hope of vastly greater benefits.

'The programme of awards is intended to call attention to a variety of persons who have found new ways to increase man's love of God or understanding of God.

'We hope that this will cause many other people to volunteer as helpers in each new and fruitful project. We hope that each such project will attract generous financial support if we help it to become better known. Thereby over the years the benefits for the winner may be vastly greater than just £34,000.*

*Increased in 1976 to £50,000.

'The programme is intended to bring much greater benefits to others than to the winner or his project. Longfellow said: "Lives of great men oft remind us that we can make our lives sublime." We hope to encourage the publication of books and articles about the winner which may inspire many others to devote their lives also to original spiritual endeavours of their own. This inspirational benefit may be of special help to bright young people.

'The *greatest* benefits of all may be received by millions of people who gradually gain a better understanding of the infinity of God and the rich variety of religious endeavour. For example, we hope to inspire more young people to devote their lives to being useful tools in God's hands and clear channels through which His love can flow. We hope that young people in each nation will come to regard religious careers as more exciting, dynamic and varied.

'We want to help religious leaders to think of spiritual subjects as worthy of research. If a few of the Christian denominations and leaders of other faiths begin to include in the church budgets some manpower and resources for research, then members may benefit in somewhat the same way as the public generally is benefiting from the extensive research in natural sciences.

'It concerns us that the political rulers of an increasingly large number of nations are trying earnestly to prevent their people from studying religion. If the programme of prizes can call attention to an impressive variety of beneficial religious projects and sound spiritual research, then possibly some political leaders may come to think that they should not exclude their people from spiritual study. In these several ways, eventually, it is possible that hundreds of millions of people may enjoy some indirect benefit.

'Could there be some better way to bring these benefits to young people, church leaders and benighted citizens of atheistic nations? We have found no better way to influence the thoughts of people for their own good than a programme of prizes which highlights and calls attention to a variety of original and fruitful spiritual projects.

'When meditating and praying about this programme years ago, we first thought the annual prize should be for progress in Christianity. Some of the best Christian leaders have advised us to design the programme so that all worshippers of every faith can feel a personal participation in this programme. Just as the people of Sweden feel a participation in a prize programme which calls attention to original work in literature and natural science, so we hope that the people of nations with British heritage will feel a participation in this programme which calls attention to a variety of spiritual progress. Accordingly the prizes are awarded each year in London and the amount is stated in Sterling. If the programme of prizes is to do much good and be influential it must be respected. The willingness of His Royal Highness Prince Philip to award the Prize, just as the royal family in Sweden awards the Swedish prizes, is a very great help in the programme. In deciding the amount of the prize we hope to convey the feeling that spiritual progress is no less important than progress in medicine or chemistry. Some of us think that to increase man's love of God and man's understanding of God is more important than all else combined. No doubt the programme can be improved. The wisdom of all is sought in trying to make the programme more beneficial. "Our constant prayer should be, Dear Lord, to do some good to Thine for Thee."

'*The Idea of Progress*

'This is not a prize for religion. It is a prize for progress. It might not be appropriate to give a prize for saintliness. Selection would be difficult indeed when the nominees come from every major faith. Instead the prize is for progress in religion. We wish to help in focussing attention on men and projects not widely known.

'For a long, long time we have been concerned that more and more of our friends tend to think of religion as old-fashioned or even obsolescent. Such concept is widespread in universities; and therefore some of the brightest young people turn to other careers.

'People are well-informed about progress in natural science. It appears that progress in natural science is geometric. But in religion progress is not so apparent. Part of the problem may be that church organizations do not yet devote substantial resources to research. We hope to have some influence on that. Also, it may be that there are multitudes of great new spiritual advances not yet widely known. Inspired persons with original spiritual concepts have not been recognized sometimes until long after death. In the four corners of the earth new religious organizations are born and works of charity and love started which are not widely understood until generations later. If we can help to call public attention to a few of these wonderful projects, people may begin to think of religion as exciting and dynamic. Leading thinkers recognize that spirit is more basic for life than even nuclear physics. But it is conceivable that God is ready to reveal Himself to those who seek by means of spiritual research even more than those who seek by astronomy and physics.

'About fifty years ago the Chief of Research at General Electric Laboratories in the U.S. said that when the great discoveries of the twentieth century go down in history they will not be in the realm of the natural sciences but in the realm of the spirit. Now fifty years later we wonder if he was right. Science discoveries are numerous and obvious. Possibly one of the reasons is that in the U.S. alone over thirty billion dollars a year is spent for scientific research but only a trickle for spiritual research.

'Some religious authors still tend to think of life as a repetition of cycles. A few are beginning to think of life not as a revolving wheel but as progress illustrated by an arrow pointing upward. No one knows enough about life or spirit. We need to seek and to learn with humility and diligence. We hope that this programme of prizes will encourage research by calling attention to a wide variety of new ideas and new projects in each major faith.

'Each year as the judges consider which nominees should be selected for the award, they consider not only new concepts of spirit but also new organizations, new methods of evangelism and new ways of communicating God's wisdom and infinite love.

'Some further thoughts

'Even the most intelligent scholar knows less than one per cent of God's infinite nature and the universe He is creating. God is infinite and we are very finite. Time, space, mass and energy are limits of our lives. God is not bound thusly, God is infinite and eternal. God created these and much more; but does He live outside time, space, mass and energy? Or rather is each a part of Him?

'It is sad to say, that for countless centuries religion has often led to strife. One reason may be that sometimes a church tends to think it knows all about God. Therefore any contrary belief must be false. Surely a God so small that He can be understood completely by any church is not God at all. If we can influence people to understand what it means to say "God is infinite", then we may help to diminish religious strife.

'It is difficult for a tree to describe completely a human; but it is even more difficult for a human to describe God. To most children, the word reality appears to mean what we can see and touch. Many of us never outgrow this narrow and egotistical viewpoint. One of the reasons why it is difficult for men to become channels for the flow of God's love and wisdom is the egocentric concept that we know all about God. Some are so egocentric as to think the tiny piece they found excludes any validity for the tiny piece found by another searcher on the other side of the earth. If this programme of awards can help people to understand better the meaning of infinity, not only may it reduce religious strife but also it may cause a better understanding of the importance of God. God is not only creator and governor but maybe God is the only reality. We should not speak of God as if He were a person separate from us. An ocean wave is temporary and it is not the ocean; but it is a little part of the ocean. Even so man can be thought of as a little part of God.

'Recently, Teilhard de Chardin, a palaeontologist and priest, helped man to understand evolution as a method by which God creates. Possibly his theology of evolution may be supplemented soon by a theology of galaxies and other theologies formulated by respected scientists. That is why it is possible that the panel of judges will include natural scientists and why scientists may be nominated as possible award winners. In fact Otto von Hapsburg has said: "We now see the natural scientists opening up the door directly to the supernatural. Everybody who has the opportunity of getting in touch with top scientists knows that there is practically not a single atheist left among them."

'The opening up of religious thought to a wider vision of God's infinity may be the major benefit of the awards programme. If we learn to be humble on the subject of what we know about God, then we may be in a better position to learn from each other. It should be expected that different concepts of God will spring up and become meaningful in different continents.

'We do not seek to encourage syncretism. We seek rather to focus attention on the wide variety of highlights in present-day religious thought and work. We seek not a unity of denominations or a unity of world religions, but rather we seek to encourage understanding of the benefits of diversity. This programme does not hope to reconcile great visions with each other, because it may be more productive if each group pursues separately its own great inspiration and vision. We hope to attract attention to the variety of good works and concepts born in each major faith. Surely we can learn from each other, because it may be more productive if each group pursues separately its own great inspiration and vision. We hope to attract attention to the variety of good works and concepts born in each major faith. Surely we can learn from each other. Those who study humility and admit that they are sinners can see clearly the need for increasing man's love of God and man's understanding of God.

' "The fruit of the spirit is love, joy, peace, longsuffering, gentleness, goodness, faith," said St Paul. By helping with the Templeton Foundation Prize for Progress in Religion, can we guide the multitudes to harvest these fruits?'

This essay shows not only the width and depth of John Templeton's thought but also his impassioned concern that mankind may come to a clear understanding of God.

John Templeton was born in the small Tennessee town of Winchester on 29th November, 1912. Louise Davis, a journalist of *The Tennessean*, a Nashville daily, wrote of her visit to his home in the Bahamas:

'. . . he has established an annual award of at least $88,400 — the Templeton Foundation Prize — already called the "Nobel Prize of Religion".

'Given for the first time last April at impressive ceremonies in London, the Templeton Prize went to an Albanian peasant, Mother Teresa, who founded a new order of nuns to minister to the lepers of Calcutta and to other suffering poor in under-developed regions of the world.

'*Who will win* the second award, to be presented in London the Wednesday before Easter, is anybody's guess at this moment. He or she may represent any religion — Christian or Jew, Muslim or Buddhist or Hindu. . . .

' "We are not looking for saintliness, but for some kind of progress in the field of religion," Templeton said. "The winner of the Templeton Prize must do something that has not been done before — something that could not have been done by an atheist.

' "Astronomers, pushing outward to new frontiers in the universe, are discovering God. It is conceivable that the

Templeton Prize could go to a natural scientist — for his work in discovering God's plan for evolution.

' "The Prize has to do with the excitement of new discoveries of God's love."

'The Prize, obviously, is not to set spiritual leaders competing. The purpose is, by spotlighting the winner, to focus attention on what is creative in religion. It is to encourage the young to realize what frontiers lie ahead in spiritual understanding, to the excitement of the spiritual world.

'Templeton, born in an exceptional family of individualists in Winchester, Tennessee, on November 29, 1912, lives in the Bahamas. His home, on a wooded hill, surrounded by white-columned porticoes on all four sides, commands a view of the sea from three sides.

'. . . Templeton enjoys the lush growth of bougainvillea and orchids, hibiscus and poinsettias, citrus and banana trees and coconut palms flourishing in the garden surrounding his home.

'In December, tropical breezes drifting off the ocean beyond the golf course stir cut flowers on a table on the veranda. In the white marble foyer and the white carpetted parlour, tall white shutters filter out the blistering sun through windows that reach from floor to ceiling.

'. . . How did he switch from business to religion? From a highly successful career as investment counsellor to a trailblazing career as spiritual innovator?

'In a sense, Templeton said, the two interests grew along together. All of his life, he has been interested in "everything".

'Templeton, whose grandmother's brother, Albert S. Marks, was governor of Tennessee from 1879 to 1881, grew up in a household so popping with ideas that he cannot remember a dull moment.

'His mother saw to that.

' "When my brother or I were interested in any subject, our mother would send away for books on the subject,"

Templeton said, glancing at the mounted butterflies on the wall.

' "I studied entomology when I was six to eight years old. I learned not only about butterflies, but about the plants that attracted them. Then Mother turned one area of her flower garden over to me. I experimented with plants that would attract butterflies."

Even today, Templeton, between frequent business trips to Switzerland, England, Japan and Canada (headquarters for his investment firm), experiments with plants in his garden.

' "Our garden is not planted in the usual way," Templeton said. . . . "We planted one of everything. We have forty varieties of hibiscus, and eight varieties of bougainvillea. We have fourteen varieties of citrus trees and many poinsettias. The variety makes the garden so much more interesting."

He no longer mounts butterflies, but as a boy he found they made excellent gifts. And as a boy he discovered the fun of taking old cars apart and putting them back together again.

' "One day, when I was playing in a hay barn, I saw an abandoned car — a 1917 Ford," Templeton said. "The farmer sold it to me for ten dollars. Soon I found another one of that same model and paid ten dollars for that. My friends in the eighth grade would come home from school with me to work on those cars.

' "We took the parts off one car to make the other work, and finally got it to run. About every third try, we could get that car to run all the way to Cowan. That was our test. If a car got to Cowan (five miles away), it was in pretty good condition."

'. . . But there were other cars, other trips from his earliest memories of Winchester. Templeton's father, Harvey Templeton of Winchester, was a lawyer, a cotton merchant who also dealt in seeds and fertilizer. In 1918, when John Templeton was six years old, cotton prices went sky-high, he said. His father decided to buy a car and hit the Dixie Highway for a family vacation in Florida.

' "Father sent off to Chicago for a Blue Book, with instructions on how to get to Florida," Templeton said. "It took two days to get from Winchester to Chattanooga, and seven more days to get to St Petersburg."

' "That Blue Book had directions like: 'Take the gravel road to the big oak tree, drive three hundred yards past the tree and turn left at the green barn,' Harvey said."

'The snows of that bitter winter had left the roads a slippery ooze. And travel meant getting stuck many times a day. At some points the water was so high that the road was hidden, Harvey Templeton said, and his father and uncle would get out and "wade the river to find where the bridge came out to the road".

'*On later expeditions*, in the 1920's, the family drove to California and New York in open touring cars, camping out every night.

' "Mother decreed a twenty-five-mile-an-hour speed limit, and we stuck to it," Harvey said.

'. . . But Joe Handly, an executive of National Life and Accident Insurance Company and a cousin of the Templeton brothers, used to spend every summer at the hospitable Winchester home, and he has other memories of John.

'. . . When the two Handly brothers, Joe and the late Avery Handly visited their Templeton cousins, the four boys would load their fishing poles and rifles into an old 1922 Buick and take off for camping expeditions along the banks of the Elk river.

' "John was a good swimmer," Handly said. "He was quiet, sensible, but lots of fun. Once when Avery took off on a risky swim over the rapids, John worried. He would watch out for younger children.

' "Sometimes we would race old cars across the fields, down by the river. We never ran out of things to do with the Templeton boys."

'The Templeton home in Winchester was a rock house on a five-acre plot at the edge of town — some five blocks from the courthouse square. In front of the house stretched a 150-foot long stone wall where petunias bloomed all summer, and in the back was a huge vegetable garden.

'John Templeton still owns that house. His brother Harvey owns the house next door, where their grandfather, a physician who served in the Confederate Army, lived. His old-fashioned remedies brought them through childhood illnesses, and Handly remembers his mother's story of the time she visited there and found the baby John desperately ill.

'. . . The only thing the Handly brothers disliked about visiting their Templeton cousins in Winchester was the rigid schedule of church on Sundays. John's mother and her sister were devoted members of the Cumberland Presbyterian Church there, and they seldom missed a service.

'*John Templeton*, in his picture-pretty house on the 2,000-acre grounds of Lyford Cay Club near Nassau, spoke affectionately of those days in the little country church. He loved it, even as his mother did.

'Did he ever think of going into the ministry?

' "Once," Templeton answered. "Briefly."

'That was when he was sixteen years old, and the church asked him to serve as Sunday School superintendent. He took his duties seriously. But it was not until he was forty years old and living in Englewood, N.J., that he taught a Sunday School class. That year as superintendent never quite lost its influence.

'But more immediate problems soon absorbed him. . . . John had always planned to go to Yale, and then suddenly the Depression wiped out his father's earnings. John's father could not send him to Yale.

'Joe Handly told the story of John Templeton's determination to make his own way at Yale. Templeton sold magazines as a door-to-door salesman, covering much of the farmland of Indiana in the summer after high school graduation to make two hundred dollars.

'His mother expanded her vegetable garden that summer and sold enough to make another two hundred.

' "With that four hundred dollars, John entered Yale and earned his way by scholarships, summer vacation jobs and jobs as dormitory manager to pay his entire way through Yale," Handly said. "He not only paid his expenses but came out three hundred dollars ahead and graduated with honours — Phi Beta Kappa and a Rhodes Scholarship for two years graduate study at Oxford University in England."

'As an undergraduate in economics at Yale, Templeton — victim of a devastating Depression — was struck by the little information available to determine the actual value of stock. He decided to make that his particular study in the business world, and on the basis of that study, he soon became one of the nation's valued financial experts.

'But at Oxford he made lasting friendships — some of which led him to step further toward his fortune. Among his best friends at Balliol College, Oxford, was another Rhodes scholar, Dr Frederic Tremaine Billings — then of Pennsylvania but for many years a prominent physician in Nashville and teacher at Vanderbilt School of Medicine.

'Dr Billings remembers Templeton as a determined young man who entered whole-heartedly into the social life at Oxford — faculty teas, the theatre and opera in London, vacation trips throughout England and the continent.

'Dr Billings remembers the expeditions that Templeton took across the English countryside in search of oil — with their good friend, a fellow Rhodes scholar, George C. McGhee, then of Oklahoma. McGhee, who has since made a vast fortune in oil and has served as ambassador to Turkey and West Germany, said in a telephone interview from Washington last week that he was not actually expecting to strike oil in England.

' "The oil soundings in England were my research project,"

McGhee said. "The purpose was to map the area, to solve certain geological problems."

'McGhee and his friend Templeton would set out across the countryside in a truck outfitted with seismographical equipment, to measure vibrations from underground blasts McGhee set off. Other students regarded it as a marvellous lark and Dr Billings has pictures of the truck, McGhee and Templeton to this day.

'*Templeton and McGhee*, on vacations from Oxford, toured Spain and Italy together, and Templeton made an "excellent companion, light-hearted, very social, very popular among our group," McGhee said.

'And then the two struck oil together — not in England, but in Texas, after their graduation from Oxford. They worked for the National Geophysical Company to make seismic surveys for oil. McGhee was vice-president of the company and Templeton treasurer.

' "Our oil business was successful indeed, and John bought an investment counselling firm in New York," McGhee said. "His intense application, his great determination and perseverance, his extreme purposefulness made it obvious that he would be successful. He showed intense concentration on whatever he undertook. He couldn't miss."

'In 1937, the year after his graduation, Templeton married Judith Folk, a Nashville girl whom he had met at Monteagle. And McGhee was best man at the wedding, at Christ Episcopal Church here.

'The Templetons had three children. John Marks, now a surgeon in Philadelphia; Anne Dudley, working on her M.D.; and Christopher Winston, studying to become an Episcopal minister. In 1951, Templeton's wife was killed in a bicycle accident at Bermuda, and the three Templeton children often spent their summers in Tennessee with their uncle and aunt, Harvey and Jewel Templeton of Winchester. Mrs Templeton would gather up some of her five children and some of John Templeton's children and take them on cross-country camping trips.

25

' "We hiked and camped in the Grand Tetons, and had great adventures together," Jewel Templeton said recently. 'Then in 1958 John Templeton married for the second time. His second wife, Mrs Irene Reynolds Butler, who had two children by a former marriage. So the Butler children and the Templeton children became one big family, and Templeton calls them "our five".

'*At vacation time*, John Templeton and his pretty blonde wife, Irene, began visiting many parts of the world with the idea of choosing one as a permanent home.

' "I have always liked the South," Templeton said as he sat in his Gone-With-the-Wind house on the lush Bahamian hilltop. "We decided on this island nine years ago, and borrowed ideas from many Tennessee homes when we built this home four years ago."

'The house, elegant to the last detail, is actually quite simple and compactly arranged inside. But the lofty Greek columns that surround it make it a landmark on the Bahamian landscape.

'. . . In a way, his effort to bring attention to the spiritual world now is to make up for the years he had to devote almost wholly to developing seven investment firms.

' "In my years of developing the investment firms, my time for research into spiritual matters was so limited that I want to make up for those years," he said.

' "My major activity is in religious work now. I plan to devote most of the rest of my life to spiritual work."

'Templeton himself had left the Cumberland Presbyterian Church when he moved to Englewood, N.J., because there was no church of that faith there. He became a member of the United Presbyterian Church, U.S.A. ("Northern Presbyterian"), chairman of trustees of Princeton Theological Seminary and active in many facets of church work.

'And then something happened that turned him toward establishing the "Nobel Prize of Religion".

' "About fifteen years ago, I became concerned with the numbers of friends who thought of religion as old-fashioned or obsolete," Templeton said. "I wanted them to know more about the exciting things that are being done in different religions today."

'At first Templeton thought in terms of Christian religions, but he became convinced that all religions had much to contribute to an understanding of God.

' "Since none of us knows one per cent of what there is to know about God, we must keep trying now approaches," he said, sitting very straight, in concentration. "I take the humble approach. Man is so tiny in God's infinite nature that we must suppose that each religious group finds some different aspect, like the blind men describing the elephant."

'Templeton is not interested in bringing all faiths or denominations together.

' "I am a great believer in diversity," he said. "People ask if I am trying to discover what elements are common to all faiths. Not at all.

' "It is more fruitful to discover rich diversity than to discover the least common denominator. I am not trying to minimize, but to enlarge humanity's outlook."

'Templeton's wife is a Christian Scientist, and Templeton is interested in faith healing. He feels that the world is only beginning to discover the power of spiritual growth, and he is convinced that only in countries where individual freedom flourishes can new ideas and insights in religion be discovered.

'*He welcomes* all new religious groups — Jesus Freaks included.

' "Their existence indicates that all human beings have a need for spiritual knowledge," Templeton said. "Most of the new groups will die out, but progress comes by having new methods tried.

' "Those that prove fruitful may be God's way of bringing more understanding. Most will perish, but some will survive. They will be known by their fruit."

27

'Templeton, a student of various religions and philosophies, does not aim his Templeton prize at archeological studies or reinterpretations of old theologies. He is interested in discovering new frontiers.

' "Among the Catholics, the Jews, the Protestants, in the history of all religions, there is always change," he said. "Some changes are good. Some bring decay."

' "The Pharisees did not approve of Christ. The Catholics did not approve of Martin Luther. The conflicts in the world of worshippers are often valuable."

'When Templeton first thought of setting up a prize that would do for religion what the Nobel Prize does for literature and the sciences, he planned to provide for the Templeton Prize in his will. But the more he thought of it, the more he was convinced that he should get on with the work while he was living.

'Now sixty-one, Templeton is in the thick of Templeton Prize business. Surprisingly, the headquarters for the religious award are in Belfast, Ireland — because that is the home city of the man whom Templeton chose to administer it.

'A committee of nine judges — some of the top religious leaders of the world — made the decision on last year's winner. Templeton himself carefully stayed out of the decision-making process.

'Some two thousand scholars and religious leaders from over the world were invited to make nominations, and the twelve top contenders were a notable group.

'. . . "Dictatorship stifles spiritual development," he said. "New spiritual understanding comes where there is the greatest individual freedom. . . . It doesn't appear there will be a chance for religion in Russia."

'Templeton, who is stimulated by intimate business contact with many lands, grabs at every moment on planes or at home to read about what is going on in the spiritual world. He may some day write a book on what he calls "the humble approach" to God.

'*He likes to entertain* people of similar interest, including some of the spiritual and business leaders of the world, and he treasures yearly visits to Tennessee friends and relatives.

'But he and his wife send no Christmas greetings. Instead they send Thanksgiving cards. This year they had their Thanksgiving card printed on pumpkin-coloured paper and imprinted with a poem on "God's gift to mankind", beginning :

> ' "God gave you this day to do just as you would.
>   You can throw it away — or do some good."

'Mrs Templeton, in trim white pants and cerise blouse, served coffee in their living room as she explained that they found Thanksgiving greetings more meaningful than Christmas cards. John Templeton, smiling his agreement, summed it up :

' "We send Thanksgiving cards," he said, "because thanking is one of the keys to opening up our spiritual growth. And spiritual growth is our goal."

chapter three

THE JUDGES

The first panel of judges highlighted the international dimension of the Prize and also set a pattern for representatives of the major faiths to take a leading part in deciding the recipient. This is seen in the person of *The Reverend Dr Eugene Carson Blake* who, as General Secretary of the World Council of Churches, brought a wealth of expertise in international co-operation and inter-faith dialogue to the Prize. At that time the World Council brought together two hundred and fifty-five churches in some ninety countries and was the forum for a large part of Christendom. Prior to his appointment to the WCC in 1966, Dr Blake was the Chief Executive Officer of the United Presbyterian Church in the U.S.A. A widely travelled churchman, he has led a quest for greater understanding of God in international affairs and for peace with justice in areas of conflict. Born in the U.S.A. in 1906, he has received numerous university and state awards since graduating from Princeton University in 1928. Since 1951 he has been a national and international figure. Familiar to millions through coverage in *The New York Times*, *Time* magazine, *U.S. News* and *World Report*, Dr Blake is best known for his proposal to create a new church 'truly catholic, truly evangelical and truly reformed,' presented in a sermon at Grace Cathedral (Episcopal) in San Francisco at the invitation of Bishop James Pike in 1960. He blazed a trail that will be marked in religious history as the era when Christianity opened its doors to the modern world and began to break down old distinctions between the sacred and the secular. Among Dr Blake's publications are : 'He is the Lord of All' and 'The Church in the Next Decade'

India's National Scholar and leading authority on Hinduism, *Professor Suniti Kumar Chatterji*, brought an eastern mind to the distinguished panel of judges. Born in Sibpur, Howrah, in 1890, he has been Emeritus Professor of Comparative Philology at Calcutta University since 1952, and was a Visiting Professor at the University of Pennsylvania (1951-52). He has been Chairman of the Upper House of West Bengal State Legislature and, since 1965, National Professor of India in the Humanities. He has participated in various learned societies including: Sengiya Sahitya Parishad (Linguistic Society of India), of which he was President; the Asiatic Society of Bengal, of which he is a former President; the Société Asiatique of Paris; the American Oriental Society; the Norwegian Academy of Sciences; the Royal Siam Society; the Ecole Française de l'Extrême Orient; the Linguistic Society of America; the Society of Arts and Sciences of Utrecht; he is a Fellow of the Indian Council for Cultural Relations; President of Sahitya Academy, New Delhi; President of the International Phonetics Association, London; and has been honoured by a number of Indian universities. His publications include : *Origin and Development of the Bengali Language* (1926); *Dvipamaya Bharal* (1940); *Indo-Aryan Indo-Mongoloids* (1951, 1974); *Africanism* (1960); *Indianism and the Indian Synthesis* (1962); *Languages and Literature of Modern India* (1964); *Dravidian; People, Language and Culture of Orissa* (1966); *Balts and Aryans* (1968); *India and Ethiopia* (1969);

World Literature and Tagore (1971); *Iranianism* (1972); *Jayadera* (1974).

Distinguished authority on intricate international legal matters and representative of one of the movements within Islam, *Sir Muhammad Zafrulla Khan*, made a notable contribution to the Prize. Born 6th February, 1893, Sir Zafrulla Khan was a Barrister-at-Law (Lincoln's Inn, London) before becoming an Advocate in Sialkot, Punjab (1914-16); he practised at Lahore High Court (1916-35); and was a member of the Punjab Legislative Council (1916-35); he was a delegate to the Indian Round Table Conferences of 1930, 1931 and 1932; and to the Joint Select Committee of Parliament on Indian Reforms (1933). He has been President of the All-India Muslim League; member of the Governor-General's Executive Council; and was leader of the Indian delegation to the Assembly of the League of Nations in 1939. He has also been Agent-General of the Government of India in China, Judge in the Federal Court of India; Constitutional Adviser to H.H. Ruler of Bhopal; Leader of the Pakistan delegation to the UN General Assembly (September-November 1947). In the Government of Pakistan, 1947, he was Minister of Foreign Affairs and Commonwealth Relations; Leader of the Pakistan delegation to the UN Security Council on the India-Pakistan dispute (1938-54) and to sessions of the UN General Assembly (1947-54). He was also Leader of the Pakistan delegation to the San Francisco Conference on the Japanese Peace Treaty (1951); and to the SEATO Conference, Manila (1954). He became a judge at the International Court of Justice at the Hague in 1954, Vice-President (1958) and President (1970-73). His publications include : *Islam : Its Meaning for Modern Man* (1962).

Dr Margaretha Klompé as a leading Roman Catholic and former Dutch cabinet minister brought to the panel an incisive mind. Dr Klompé was born in Arnheim in 1912. She worked for many years as a teacher in Nijmegen before becoming a politician. As a member of the Netherlands delegation she attended the UN General Assemblies (1947, 1948, 1950 and 1952). She was a member of the Consultative Assembly of the Council of Europe (1949-56), of the Coal and Steel Assembly (1952-56). Cabinet posts held by Dr Klompé have been: Minister of Social Welware (1956-63); Minister of Culture, Social Welfare and Education (1966-71); and Minister of State. As a leading Roman Catholic laywoman she is a member of the Pontifical Commission on Justice and Peace and President of the National Commission on Justice and Peace. She is also President of the National UNESCO Commission.

Judaism was represented by the distinguished British judge *Sir Alan Mocatta*, who is a judge of the Queen's Bench Division of the High Court. Born in 1907, Sir Alan has had an imposing legal career: since 1967 he has been a member of the Treasury Committee on Cheque Endorsement and is also a member of the Restrictive Practices Court. As a prominent member of the Anglo-Jewish community he has been Chairman of the Council of Jews' College, President of the Board of Elders of the Spanish and Portuguese Jews' Congregation (Bevis Marke).

Dr James McCord, President of Princeton Theological Seminary in New Jersey, is one of Mr Templeton's closest advisors and confidants who drafted the initial outline of the purposes and objectives of the award. A noted theologian, he is the North American Secretary of the World Alliance of Reformed Churches and was the first Chairman of the Consultation on Church Union. A member of the Commission on Faith and Order of the World Council of Churches and the first Chairman of the Department of Faith and Order of the National Council of Churches in the U.S.A.; Dr McCord is also Chairman of the Commission on Accrediting of the American Association of Theological Schools. He is the editor of *Supplementa Calviniana* and other noted books. Born in 1919, Dr McCord was educated at Austin College, New College, Edinburgh, and Harvard University.

A leading Buddhist in the person of *Lord Abbot Kosho Ohteani* from the authoritative Nishi Hongwanjni Temple made a notble contribution. He is the patriarch of the Shin Sects, one of the principal denominations of Japanese Buddhism. He became priest of Nishi Hongwanji in 1927 and Patriarch in 1935. A graduate of Tokyo University, he has written several important books including *Buddhistic Ritual in Tao Era* and *The Meaning of Being Taught*. Born in 1911, to Abbot Koymo Ohtani, he was adopted by Abbot Kozui Ohtani as his heir apparent. He is married to the elder daughter of Prince Tokudaiji.

The success of the Templeton Prize thus far is in large measure due to the personal interest taken in it by *The Right Reverend Robin Woods*, the Anglican Bishop of Worcester in England. The Bishop, born in 1914, was Archdeacon of Singapore and Vicar of St Andrew's Catheddral (1951-58); Archdeacon of Sheffield and Rector of Tankersley (1968-72); Dean of Windsor, Domestic Chaplain to the Queen and Registrar of the Most Noble Order of the Garter (1962-70); Secretary, Anglican/Methodist Commission for Unity (1965); Member, Council for the Duke of Edinburgh's Award Scheme (1968) of the Public Schools Commission (1968-70); Governor of Haileybury College; President of Queen's College, Birmingham; Chairman, Windsor Festival Council (1969), of the Churches Television Centre (since 1969) and Director of Christian Aid (since 1969).

The distinguished Anglican layman, *Lord Thurlow*, was born in 1912. He has held many posts in the British diplomatic service: he served with the UK delegation to the Paris Peace Conference (1946) and the UN General Assemblies (1946 and 1948); was Head of the Political Division, Office of the UK High Commissioner in New Delhi (1949); Advisor on External Affairs to the Governor of Gold Coast (1955); Deputy High Commissioner for the UK in Ghana (1957); Deputy High Commissioner for the UK in Canada (1958); High Commissioner for the UK in

New Zealand (1959-63), in Nigeria (1964-67); and Governor of the Bahamas (1968-73).

After serving for an initial three years Dr Blake, Dr Klompe and Lord Ohtani retired. They were followed by *Her Majesty Fabiola, Queen of the Belgians*. Her Majesty, who was born in Spain, is the Queen Consort of His Majesty King Baudouin. She belongs to a family of the Spanish aristocracy. The Queen, who before her marriage was a nurse in Madrid, pays regular visits to hospitals and charitable institutions, expressing her care towards the people who are in need of help by means of the social action of her Secretary's Office. She takes an active interest in Belgian cultural and religious affairs as well as in the problems of the developing countries.

His All Holiness Demetrios I is the 269th Archbishop of Constantinople, New Rome and Ecumenical Patriarch. He succeeded Patriarch Athenagoras I, who died in 1972. The Ecumenical Patriarch is the spiritual leader of fourteen autocephalous Orthodox churches around the world with a total of 126 million members (figure for 1975). The seat of the patriarchate is the Phanar in Istanbul. The Patriarch was born Demetrios Papadopoulos in Istanbul in 1914. From 1945 to 1950 he was Chaplain to the Greek community in Teheran where he taught classical Greek at the University. Returning to Istanbul, he became Vicar General of Ferikoy, an Istanbul suburb, and was consecrated Bishop of Eleia. In February 1972 he was named Archbishop of Imbros and Tenedos, islands at the mouth of the Dardanelles. Six months later he was chosen Ecumenical Patriarch by the fifteen metropolitans of the Holy Synod from a list of three candidates approved by the Turks. His All Holiness said after his coronation 'We wish to emphasize that we shall systematically aim to achieve pan-Orthodox unity and through it pan-Christian unity.'

The third judge to join the panel in 1974 was *Her Serene Highness Princess Poon Pismai Diskul*, a member of the royal family of Thailand. Her Serene Highness is President

35

of the World Fellowship of Buddhists, a Vice-President of the Buddhist Association of Thailand and a member of the Committee for Revision of Thai History of the Government of Thailand. She has also served as President of the Buddhist Association of Thailand, Instructor in Thai History to the former His Majesty King Ananda Mahidol. The princess's contribution to the cause of the Dhamma through these long years is best reflected in her active participation in various social functions in connexion with Buddhism. Her appointment as President of the World Fellowship of Buddhists and consequent location of the organization's headquarters in Thailand, on the decision of the seventh World Fellowship of Buddhist Conference, has revivified the organization which was then facing almost certain dissolution. She has travelled extensively on the Fellowship's behalf and her writings are well respected: *Sasaneguna* or *The Value of Religion* (for which she was awarded a prize by His Majesty King Rama VII), *My First Impression of Europe, Thai Traditions and Customs* and *A Being that is Human.*

The following year Sir Alan Mocatta, Professor Chatterji and Lord Thurlow retired. They were succeeded by: the Indian diplomat and politician *Shri Apasaheb Balasaheb Pant* who at that time was Ambassador of India to Italy. During a distinguished career he has served as Minister of Education, Aundh State, Prime Minister (1938-44); member of All-India Congress Committee (1948); Commissioner for the Government of India in British East Africa (1948-54); concurrently Consul-General in the Belgian Congo and Ruanda-Urundi (1948-1953), concurrently Commissioner in Central Africa and Nyasaland (1950-54); Officer on Special Duty, Ministry of External Affairs, New Delhi (1954-55); Political Officer, Sikkim and Bhutan, with control over Indian missions in Tibet (1955-61); Ambassador to Indonesia (1961-64), to Norway (1964-66), to U.A.R. (1966-69); High Commissioner in UK (1969-72); Ambassador to Italy and High Commissioner, Malta (1972-76);

36

delegate to the UN General Assemblies (1951, 1952 and 1965). Mr Pant's publications include: *Tensions and Tolerance* (1965); *Aggression and Violence! Ghandian Experiments to Fight Them* (1968); *Yoga* (1968); *Surya Namaskar* (1969); *A Moment in Time*.

The Reverend Dr Norman Vincent Peale has been minister of Marble Collegiate Reformed Church in New York City since 1932. He is well known in the United States and throughout the world as both a writer and a preacher. He is editor of the mass-circulation inspirational magazine *Guideposts*, though he is better known through his book *The Power of Positive Thinking*. Dr Peale is a Trustee of Ohio Wesleyan College and Union Central College, a member of the Executive Committee of the Presbyterian Ministers Fund for Life Insurance; and Mid-Century White House Conference on Children and Youth; President of the National Temperance Society and the Protestant Council of the City of New York; and a Lecturer on public affairs and personal effectiveness.

Mr Edmund Leopold de Rothschild is President of the Bank of Rothschilds and Chairman of N. M. Rothschild & Sons Ltd. Born in London in 1916, Mr de Rothschild was educated at Harrow School and Trinity College Cambridge. Outside his full business life Mr de Rothschild takes a significant role in community affairs. His particular interest is Christian-Jewish dialogue through his involvement with the Council of Christians and Jews of which he is Treasurer in Great Britain. He was Joint Treasurer of the United Kingdom for World Refugee Year and Trustee appointed by the British Government for the Freedom from Hunger Campaign. Since 1967 he has travelled extensively, seeing world leaders in an effort to relieve the plight of the refugees in the Middle East.

In 1976 Sir Zafrulla Khan, Dr McCord and the Bishop of Worcester were replaced by: *Sir Bernard Lovell*, Professor of Radio Astronomy of the University of Manchester (England) and Director of the Jodrell Bank Experimental

Station (now Nuffield Radio Astronomy Laboratories), who was a member of the Aeronautical Research Council (1955-58), and of the Science Research Council (1965-70). He was President of the Royal Astronomical Society (1969-71) and is an Honorary Fellow of the Society of Engineers, a Foreign Member of the American Academy of Arts and Sciences, an Honorary Life Member of the New York Academy and an Honorary Member of the Royal Swedish Academy. He is the holder of honorary degrees from a number of universities as well as a number of international awards, and was President of the British Association for the Advancement of Science (1975).

The Right Reverend John V. Taylor has been Bishop of Winchester (England) since January 1975. He was warden of Bishop Tucker College, Mukono, Uganda (1945-54), Research Worker with the International Missionary Council (1955-59) until becoming Africa Secretary, and later General Secretary, at the Church Missionary Society. He has published a number of books, particularly on Christian mission in Africa. He is a leading figure in the ecumenical movement and is the Prelate to the Most Noble Order of the Garter.

Mr Masakazu Echigo, who graduated in Economics from Kobe University in Japan, is the third Buddhist to be appointed to the Templeton award during the past four years. He is a leading member of the Hongwanji demonination of Japanese Buddhism and a principal Japanese industrialist. Mr Echigo, who is Chairman of C Itoh & Co. Ltd. — a major Japanese trading house, is also Director of the International Chamber of Commerce and Vice-President of the Japan Foreign Trade Council. He is also Director of a number of Japanese companies and Austrian Honorary Consul General in Osaka. In May 1971 he was awarded the second class of the Order of the Rising Sun by the Emperor of Japan. He was a recipient of the Blue Ribbon Medal from the Emperor in 1963.

chapter four

THE TRUSTEES AND
ADVISORY BOARD

Advisors to the Foundation for the Prize have been instrumental in making the award more widely known particularly through the mass media and in specialized journals in the sciences and religion.

Graham Williams, one of Australia's national journalists, pinpointed the need for such an award in Australian society and in analysing the purpose, objectives and criteria of the award aroused the Australian people to the extent that today there is a very keen interest throughout Australia. This was further evidenced when I paid a visit to Australia. The demands of press, radio and television for interviews surpassed those of any other country at that time.

Some advisors have been making more widely known the purpose and objectives of the Prize and at the same time answer any questions that may be raised where they happen to be.

William Pollard is an Episcopalian minister of the United States and has been Director of the Oak Ridge Laboratories, the nerve centre of nuclear studies in the United States. Through his relationship with scientists he has brought to the Foundation names of a number through whose achievements one can see God's creative hand at work.

Gertrud Brundin is a specialist in religious affairs in the Swedish Broadcasting Corporation. Her popular programme has done a lot to make the Prize more widely known in Sweden.

These are but three of the outstanding specialists who have advanced the idea of the award and through whom a wider audience has heard and come to hear about the progress in religion.

Advisors for the Prize over the years have been:

Dr Arthur Adams, Dean of Princeton Theological Seminary, New Jersey (USA);

Mr Martin Bailey, Editor, *AD*, an American Presbyterian magazine;

Dr Russell Barber, Religion Editor of National Broadcasting Co., New York (USA);

Mr Constantino E. Bernardez, Executive Director, South East Asia Radio Voice, Manila (Philippines);

Mr Henk Biersteker, formerly a journalist of *Dagblad Trouw*, now with IKOR, a Dutch radio and television station;

Archdeacon Murillo Bonaby of Nassau (Bahamas);

Sir Milo Butler, Governor of the Bahamas;

Dr Clayton B. Craig, formerly Director and Trustee of the Christian Science Church, Boston;

Mr George T. Delacorte, President of Delacorte Foundation (USA);

The Hon. Sir Etienne Dupuch OBE, Editor-Proprietor, *The Tribune*, Nassau (Bahamas);

The Right Reverend Michael Eldon, Bishop of Nassau (Bahamas);

The Rev'd Ted Fiske, formerly religion editor *New York Times* (USA);

Mrs Reau E. Folk Jr, radio producer, Nashville (USA);

Dr A. C. Forrest, Editor, *The United Church Observer*, Toronto (Canada);

*Dr *John M. Francis*, Senior Research Fellow in Energy Studies, Herriott-Watt University, Edinburgh (Scotland);

*Mr *Hans-Wolfgang Hessler*, Editor, *Evangelischer Pressedienst* (church news service), Frankfurt (Federal German Republic);

*The *Right Reverend Leonard Haggarty OSB*, bishop, Nassau (Bahamas);

*Dr *B. S. Hruby*, Editor, *Religion in Communist Dominated Areas*, New York (USA);

*Miss *Anneli Janhonen* of the Information Centre of the Church of Finland, Helsinki;

*The *Reverend Dr P. A. Johnson*, formerly Executive Director of the World Association for Christian Communication, now President of the Council on Religion and International Affairs (Dr Johnson served as Chairman of the Board of Advisors from the inauguration of the Prize until 1976);

*Mr *Christopher Kolade*, Director General, Nigerian Broadcasting Corporation, Lagos (Nigeria);

*The *Reverend James Lawson*, a pastor from Lome (Togo);

*Mr *Henry Luce III*, publisher of *Time*, *Fortune* and *People*, New York (USA);

*The *Reverend Dr James McCord*, President, Princeton Theological Seminary, Princeton, New Jersey (USA);

*Mr *William MacKaye*, religion editor, *Washington Post*, Washington DC (USA);

*Mr *Melville de Mellow*, Chief Producer Features (English), All India Radio, New Delhi (India);

*Mr *Svein Ottesen*, religion editor, *Aftenposten* (daily paper), Oslo (Norway);

*Dr *Arthur Peacocke*, Dean, Clare College, Cambridge (England);

*Mr *Juan Pia Jr*, General Manager, MASCOM Network (Philippines);

*Dr *William Pollard*, Episcopal Minister, Director Oak Ridge Laboratories (U.S.A.);

chapter five

MOTHER TERESA 1973

The telephone line to Calcutta was a constant crackle and after considerable tinkering by the international operator in London a quiet voice at the home of the Missionaries of Charity said Mother Teresa was in Australia for the International Eucharistic Congress and would not be returning to Calcutta for about ten days. I inquired as to Mother Teresa's itinerary and much to my relief her diary was free for the dates of the presentation in London. At the Missionaries of Charity home in Calcutta the curiosity of the sister I spoke to was aroused when I said I was from the Templeton Foundation. 'What is it?' 'What does it do?' 'Is it asking Mother to do anything?'

Ten days later the telephone again crackled and when I told Mother Teresa that the nine judges drawn from the major faiths of the world had chosen her as the first recipient of the Templeton Foundation Prize for Progress in Religion she was thrilled but not overawed and calmly said: 'It is a gift from God.'

I asked her if she would come to London to receive the award from His Royal Highness Prince Philip and a few days later she confirmed her arrangements.

This culminated a year of detailed work during which we received many nominations from the major religions of the world. However, the judges, after detailed consideration of those nominations placed before them, decided that the Prize ought to go to Mother Teresa. Malcolm Muggeridge's book, *Something Beautiful for God*, which tells the story of Mother Teresa and her work, inspired the judges whose decision caught the imagination of the world.

Tuesday morning, April 24, 1973, was eventful at London's Heathrow Airport for the arrival of the scheduled Air India Boeing jet. Senior representatives of Air India were on hand to meet Mother Teresa as she disembarked. Expecting much baggage, an Air India executive asked her for her baggage tags but Mother Teresa replied by holding up the two tiny cardboard cartons tied with string and said : 'This is my baggage.' Dressed in a simple white sari with royal blue edging and wearing a cardigan and sandals the diminutive nun, who was born in Yugoslavia of Albanian parents and educated in Ireland at the Loretto Convent, was immediately crowded by hundreds of well-wishers who had come to see her. A young Indian immigrant mother with her tiny baby hurried to the Mother of Charity to have the baby blessed — a moving sight not lost on the British press photographers — a photograph which was flashed to the world's newspapers.

Guildhall, with its centuries of tradition and its more recent memorial to Sir Winston Churchill, was packed for the evening ceremony. The large audience burst into applause as Mother Teresa took her seat on the platform beside the Lord Mayor of London who chaired the ceremony.

H.R.H. Prince Philip, in presenting the award to Mother Teresa, said : 'at first sight the idea that a prize might be able to do something for religion seems faintly absurd. A prize, in the ordinary sense, is an encouragement to succeed or recognition of some measurable achievement. A prize is usually something to be striven for.

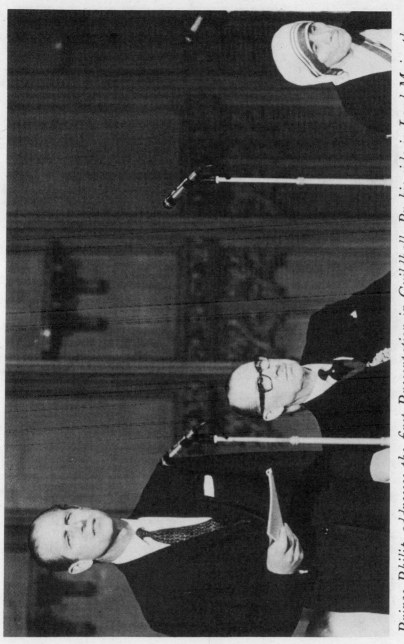

Prince Philip addresses the first Presentation in Guildhall. By his side is Lord Mais, then Lord Mayor of London.

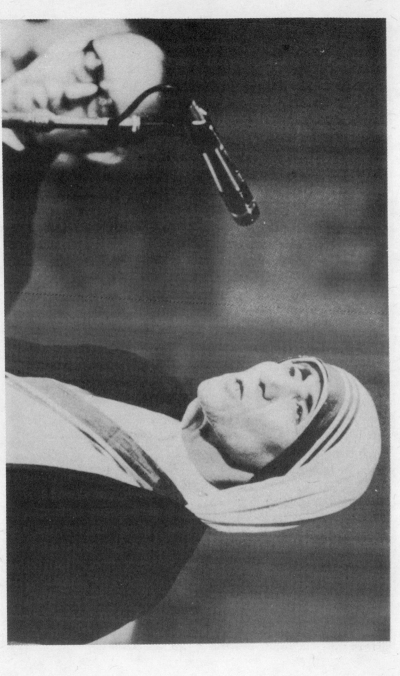

Mother Teresa addresses the Guildhall audience on receiving the First Templeton Prize from Prince Philip.

'In the case of a prize for religion the only certainty is that those who are worthy to receive it will most definitely not have striven for it. I simply cannot conceive the possibility of anyone coldly deciding to do something for religion in order to win this prize. In any case is it really possible for even the most worthy and distinguished judges to decide whether one person has done God's work better than another? I frankly admit that I was very much in two minds about this idea, even though I realized perfectly well that Mr Templeton had not conceived this as a prize in the conventional sense. . . .

'Then came the news of the person selected to receive the Prize together with a description of Mother Teresa's work, particularly among the very poor in Calcutta. I am sure that Mr Templeton will forgive me for saying so, but it is really Mother Teresa who has made this Prize work in the way it was intended.'

The Lord Mayor of London, Lord Mais, in chairing the ceremony said: 'You will know that this Prize is unique in that it crosses all traditional, religious doctrinaire barriers. It is a great pleasure therefore to welcome leaders and representatives from many religious beliefs here this evening. The judges have included Christians, of several denominations, a Hindu, a Muslim and a Buddhist, and all are noted for their interest in relations between the world religions.' The Lord Mayor further spoke of Mother Teresa's 'selfless and devoted work in Calcutta'.

The evening belonged to Mother Teresa, still dressed in her sari, cardigan and sandals, who said: 'In giving this award to me, actually it is given to the people, to all those who share with me throughout the world in the work of love, in spreading God's love amongst men.'

The simplicity and humility of Mother Teresa were again seen when the doors of Guildhall were closed and the crowds had gone home and she was saying goodbye to the judges and officials of the Foundation, when one of the sisters said: 'Mother, where is the cheque? May we see it?'

And to everyone's astonishment Mother Teresa said: 'I do not know where I left it.' Guildhall officials, amazed at such a statement, opened the historic hall and diligently retraced Mother Teresa's footsteps until they found the cheque for £34,000 lying under a chair!

The speeches of that evening will perhaps be the most significant of the awards, for a new era had dawned in the quest for a better understanding of God and of man's understanding of man.

In the programme, excerpts from Malcolm Muggeridge's book *Something Beautiful for God*, summed up the life of Mother Teresa for many: 'Doing something beautiful for God, is for Mother Teresa, what life is about. Everything, in that it is for God, becomes beautiful, whatever it may be; as does every human soul participating in this purpose, whoever he or she may be. In manifesting this, in themselves and in their lives and work, Mother Teresa and the Missionaries of Charity provide a living witness to the power and truth of what Jesus came to proclaim. His light shines in them. When I think of them in Calcutta, as I often do, it is not the bare house in a dark slum that is conjured up in my mind, but a light shining and a joy abounding. I see them diligently and cheerfully constructing something beautiful for God out of the human misery and affliction that lies around them.

'The Christian religion finds expression thus, in the love of those who love Christ, more comprehensibly and accessibly than in metaphysical or ethical statements. It is an experience rather than an ideology; grasped through the imagination rather than understood through the mind, belonging to the realm of spiritual rather than intellectual perception; reaching quite beyond the dimension of words and ideas. As St Augustine found on that wonderful occasion at Ostia with his mother shortly before she died when they were carried together to somewhere near the very presence of God, and then, returning, found words as clumsy instruments as a surgeon might find a hack-saw, or an artist a housepainter's brush — "And while we spoke of the eternal Wisdom, longing for it and straining for it with all the strength of our hearts, for one fleeting instant we reached out and touched it. Then, with a sigh, leaving our spiritual harvest bound to it, we returned to the sound of our own speech, in which each word has a beginning and an ending — far, far different from your Word, our Lord, who abides in Himself for ever, yet never grows old and gives new life to all things."

'The Christian story is simply an endless presentation of this process of the Word becoming flesh and dwelling gracefully and truthfully among us. Whether in the ultimate silence of the mystic, such as befell St Augustine and his mother — a silence that comprehends all that ever has been, will be and can be said and understood and sensed, from before the beginning of time to beyond its ending. Or in a Mother Teresa and her Missionaries of Charity going about the world and shining their light in its darkest places. Or in the splendour of artistic creation; in the great cathedrals climbing into the sky to God's greater glory; in the glowing words, the sentient stone and paint, the swelling sounds of music. Or in the solitary soul questing for truth, in the tiniest mechanism of our mortal existence, as in the universe's illimitable reaches.

'For me, Mother Teresa of Calcutta embodies Christian love in action. Her face shines with the love of Christ on which her whole life is centred, and her words carry that message to a world which never needed it so much.'

Press, radio and television were quick to appreciate that. BBC television carried from Guildhall an excerpt in its evening news which caught the imagination of the British people who are not known for such instant enthusiasm. The next day London's mass-circulation *Daily Express* carried a feature article on the 'nun with hope for the world' and Thames Television, together with London Weekend Television, two leading commercial companies in the independent network, carried seven evening programmes on the Prize and Mother Teresa.

Statement of Mr John M. Templeton

Your Royal Highness, My Lord Mayor, Your Excellencies, My Lords, Ladies and Gentlemen:

This evening, The Templeton Foundation makes the first award of its Prize for Progress in Religion. The Foundation inaugurated this programme in the historic church of Saint Bride in Fleet Street in May of last year in the hope that this programme will contribute toward increasing man's love of God and man's knowledge of God. Also, it is the hope of the Foundation that the Prize will release new and creative energies into society through better understanding of the meaning of life and a greater emphasis on the kind of dedication that brings people more into concert with the Divine Will.

God is revealing more of himself to me in many ways. We see this in God's continual creation of the atoms and the galaxies. We see it in the new experience of men and in the discoveries of scientists.

It is not surprising that men on different continents make different discoveries in their long search to understand more of God's infinite nature. Men are finding new ways to worship God — new ways to open their hearts to receive and radiate God's infinite love. We should rejoice in this rich diversity. Surely we can learn from each other.

The Templeton Foundation seeks to award its Prize each year to a person who has helped to increase our love of God, or our understanding of God. Qualities sought in awarding the Prize are originality, inspiration, creativity, innovation and effectiveness. Such contribution may involve a study, or a life, or the inspiration of a new movement in religion. Examples of this can be seen in pioneering and innovative study, in new forms of worship and devotion and in the fashioning of new and effective methods of communicating faith. Also, within the criteria for the

Prize, are the creation of new structures of understanding about the relationship of God to the universe, to the physical sciences or to the life sciences.

While the Prize has been conceived in the West with its mainly Christian tradition, persons who are representative of Buddhism, Hinduism, Islam and Judaism are also among the judges. Worthy candidates are nominated and considered for the Prize each year, from each of the world's major faiths. We know the differing theological language and doctrine between our various traditions; yet we also know that as we meet together we can be renewed within our respective traditions in our commitment to our Creator. Together we hope to share our common humanity and dignity and to express our common concern for man's spiritual well being. From a Christian point of view, this working together implies neither a denial of the uniqueness of Christ nor any loss of the Christian's own commitment to Christ, but rather a genuine Christian approach to others in a human, personal, spiritual and humble way.

Progress is needed in religion as in all other dimensions of human experience and endeavour. It is imperative that progress in religion be accelerated as progress in other dimensions takes place. A wider universe demands a deeper awareness of the spirit and of spiritual resources available to man, of the immensity of God, and of God's infinite love. Personally, I am deeply grateful to each of the nine judges who have been painstaking in their consideration of the nominees. From their several spiritual traditions, the judges reached their decision, and tonight we honour their choice. I am also grateful to the Lord Mayor and Corporation of London for welcoming us to this historic city. I am grateful to His Royal Highness, Prince Philip, for presenting this year's prize to Mother Teresa of Calcutta.

Address of The Right Hon. The Lord Mayor of London, The Lord Mais

Your Royal Highness, it is a great honour for the City of

London that the first award of the Templeton Foundation Prize for Progress in Religion should be presented in our Guildhall, and that His Royal Highness The Duke of Edinburgh has kindly consented to make this presentation.

His Royal Highness requires no introduction in Guildhall but we do thank you, Sir, for finding time in your busy life to be here this evening.

It gives me special pleasure to welcome, on behalf of you all, Mr and Mrs John Templeton. Without Mr Templeton's imagination and generosity there would be no prize — and although we well know that that would in no way have changed Mother Teresa's dedication, it is fitting that the field of Religious Progress should be recognized and the Templeton Foundation Award will, we all trust, inspire mankind to further the quest for that quality of life which mirrors its religious ideals.

Mr Templeton is no stranger in this country. He was a Rhodes scholar at Oxford and gained there the degree of Master of Arts (in law) to add to his many academic distinctions, and we are glad that it is here in England that he will see his first prize awarded.

You will know that this Prize is unique in that it crosses all traditional, religious doctrinaire barriers. It is a great pleasure therefore to welcome leaders and representatives from many religious beliefs here this evening. The judges have included Christians of several denominations — a Hindu, a Muslim, and a Buddhist, and all are noted for their interest in relations between the world religions. Not all are able to be present tonight but of their number we welcome the Reverend Dr Blake, (former) General Secretary of the World Council of Churches; Dr Woods, the Anglican Bishop of Worcester, and Lord Thurlow, a distinguished Anglican layman.

I believe that the City of London is an appropriate setting for this ceremony. Going back in time until the City of London (as we know it) was London, we have a long tradition of liberal learning. The earliest schools were attached to the City Churches and there was from the first a special concern for 'poor scholars'. Later, individual citizens and guilds founded schools all over the country, often extensions of an original city religious foundation. Thus, we have helped to prepare men's minds for — to quote from the Objectives of the Templeton Foundation — 'a deeper spiritual awareness and a better understanding of the meaning of life'.

In another field too, the City's activities are relevant. So many of the old foundations jealously preserved here are of a charitable nature—as is the Foundation of Mr Templeton. Our charitable foundations have, over the centuries, helped great numbers of people — often without regard to religion or race — and it is a pleasure therefor to be the host, so to speak, for this admirable 'newcomer'.

I have said nothing so far about the most important person here tonight — Mother Teresa. This is because I know that His Royal Highness is looking forward to speaking about her shortly — but I do not wish to take advantage of my position as Chairman in making a personal tribute. I have read—and seen on television—of Mother Teresa's selfless and devoted work in Calcutta. I know that you, Mother Teresa, would be the last to seek recognition but you are the first to deserve it.

It has been a special privilege for me to take the Chair this evening when you are to be honoured and I would like, Mother, to add my sincere personal congratulations and gratitude for your life work and its so well deserved recognition.

Address of H.R.H. The Duke of Edinburgh

At first sight the idea that a prize might be able to do something for religion seems faintly absurd. A prize, in the ordinary sense, is an encouragement to succeed or recognition of some measurable achievement. A prize is usually something to be striven for.

In the case of a prize for religion the only certainty is that those who are worthy to receive it will most definitely not have striven for it. I simply cannot conceive the possibility of anyone coldly deciding to do something for religion in order to win this prize. In any case is it really possible for even the most worthy and distinguished judges to decide whether one person has done God's work better than another? I frenkly admit that I was very much in two minds about this idea, even though I realized perfectly well that Mr Templeton had not conceived this as a prize in the conventional sense.

I respected the intention of his imaginative proposal and I have every confidence in the judges, but I doubted whether it would work.

Then came the news of the person selected to receive the prize together with a description of Mother Teresa's work, particularly among the very poor in Calcutta. I am sure that Mr Templeton will forgive me for saying so, but it is really Mother Teresa who has made this prize work in the way it was intended.

The usual procedure on these occasions is to congratulate the prize winner. I don't think there is any question of doing that today. In this case, we can only be thankful for Mother Teresa's work and grateful to the judges for drawing our attention to it. It is Mr Templeton and the judges who are to be congratulated for having Mother Teresa accept the Templeton Prize.

I have already said that I had misgivings about this idea. The misgivings have gone and I freely admit that my first reactions were wrong. However, they have been replaced by even greater misgivings about what I am supposed to be doing here. The sheer goodness which shines through Mother Teresa's life and work can only inspire humility, wonder and admiration. What more is there to be said when the deeds speak so loudly for themselves?

There is nothing I can say about Mother Teresa, but I think there is much to be learned from her example. I believe that the lesson which we should learn from this

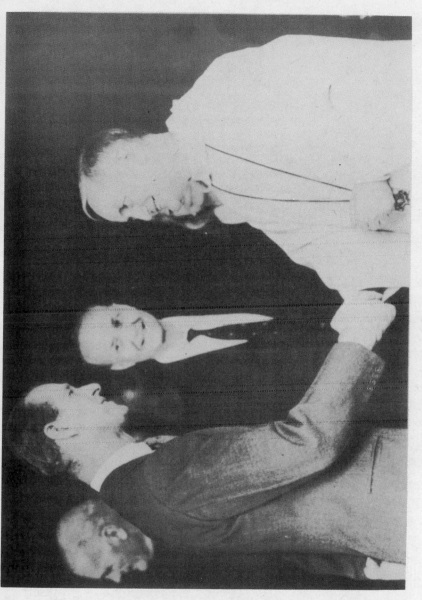

Prince Philip congratulating Brother Roger of Taize on receiving the 1974 award.

Brother Roger at home in Taize.

occasion is a very simple one and a very old one. It is just that the strength of a person's faith is measured by his actions. St Paul puts it this way: 'What use for a man to say he has faith when he does nothing to show it?' Mother Teresa would not have lived this life and done this work, and could not have done it, without an overpowering faith. Indeed I do not believe there is any other way of measuring faith except through daily action and behaviour. No ceremonies, no protestations, no displays, no routines of prayer and no theorising can compare with the smallest act of genuine and practical compassion as a true reflection of personal faith.

I think there is a very natural tendency for many people to look upon God as the all-powerful creator and then to work downwards looking for his influence on events and for his continuing control of the world. I suspect that it might be better to begin with the evidence of the lives of people like Mother Teresa — that is if there is anyone quite like her — and to work from that evidence towards a better understanding of the power of God. Their work and achievements are really beyond what can reasonably be expected from members of the genus Homo in the strictly biological scientific sense.

Yet they are ordinary flesh and blood; the difference is their motivation, their inspiration, the driving force within them. The nature of that force can be seen quite clearly in the works which it inspires and if it is capable of so transforming an individual it must be very powerful indeed. It is in the lives of such people that the nature and influence of God is to be recognized, and it is there that it should be expected, and not in inconsistent intervention in the process of mechanism of nature.

A tremendous power has entered into Mother Teresa. It might, of course, have found her anyway. But I suspect that she was moved to seek this power of God and it was able to reach her because she was brought up within the Christian tradition. It was through the influence of a devout family and community that she became aware of the idea of God as loving and compassionate. It was this introduction which opened up the line of communication and made it possible for the message to reach her. I hope that her example and her Order in their turn may be the means by which the Christian idea is made alive and apparent to a great many people.

Not everyone exposed to the Christian tradition is going to get the message quite in this way but the chances of getting any useful message at all, without some experience of a religious environment and without any will to serve God, is very small indeed. The idea that the world can easily do without religious inspiration betrays a very limited outlook. The extent to which humanity has been converted from groups of superior animals to peaceful and compassionate communities is largely due to the vision and to the example of the great religious leaders.

If that process towards more civilized living is to go on, many more people will have to be exposed to religious thought, so that some, at least, can open up a line of communication which may eventually allow a message to get through. Those who receive a message, whether weak or strong, will have to live and work by it every moment of their lives.

Without the chance of receiving the message, the most well meaning, energetic and intelligent human being is really no more than a humble bee trapped in a bottle. Without the sort of moral inspiration which is the whole purpose of religion, all our institutions become rather pointless. Why bother to educate? Is it possible to have a purposeless culture? What is the point of justice? Why be concerned about the weak and helpless, isn't honesty just a vain hope?

Mother Teresa has shown by her life what people can do when the faith is strong. By any standards what she has done is good. The world today is desperately in need of this sort of goodness, this sort of practical compassion. I hope this prize will help Mother Teresa in her work, but I also hope that everyone who hears about this event, and perhaps as a result of it learns a little about the life and work of Mother Teresa, will gain a better understanding of what is meant by faith.

Address of Mother Teresa of Calcutta

Dear Co-workers in Christ, we are here today to thank God for giving grace to Mr Templeton to accept, to give of his best to be spent for the glory of God, to have accepted that vision, to appreciate the gift of God. And so today and now we thank God that he had the courage to give, to be spent for the glory of God, the wealth that he had received so generously from God.

In giving this award to me, actually it is given to the people, to all those who share with me throughout the world in the work of love, in spreading God's love amongst men. Actually, we are touching His body, it is the hungry Christ that we are feeding, it is the naked Christ that we are clothing, it is the homeless Christ that we are giving shelter, and it is not only just hunger for bread, and naked-ness for clothes, and homelessness for a house made of bricks, but Christ today is hungry in our poor people, and even in the rich, for love, for being cared for, for being wanted, for having someone to call their own. Today, like before, when Jesus comes among His own and His own don't know Him, He comes in the broken bodies of our poor, He comes even in the rich who are being suffocated with their riches, in the loneliness of their hearts, and there is no one to love them.

And here Jesus comes to you and to me and very often, very, very often, we pass Him by. Here in England and other places, in Calcutta, in Melbourne, New York we find lonely people who are known by the number of their room. Where are we there? Do we really know that there are some people, maybe next door to us, maybe there is a blind man who would be happy if you would read the newspaper for him, maybe there is a rich person who has no one to visit him, he has plenty of other things, he is nearly drowned in that, but there is not that touch and he needs your touch. Some time back a very rich man came to our place and he told me, 'Please, either you or somebody, come to my house. I am nearly half-blind and my wife is nearly mental; and our children have all gone abroad, and we are dying of loneliness, we are longing for the loving sound of a human voice' — loving sound!

And in one of the places in Melbourne I visited an old man and nobody ever knew that he existed. And I saw his room in a terrible state, and I wanted to clean his house, his room, and he kept on saying 'I'm all right!' but I repeated the same word, 'You will be more all right if you will allow me to clean your place', and at the end he allowed me. And there in that room there was a beautiful lamp covered with dirt of many years, and I asked him 'Why do you not light your lamp?' Then I asked him, 'Will you light the lamp if the Sisters come to see you?' He said, 'Yes, if I hear a human voice I will do it.' And the other day he sent me word, 'Tell my friend the light she has lit in my life is still burning.'

This is the people that we must know, this is Jesus yesterday, and today and tomorrow, and you and I, we must know who they are, that knowledge will lead us to love them and love to service. Let us not be satisfied with just giving money, money is not enough, money can be got, but they need, they need your hearts to love them. And with this award of spreading religion, to me and to you the religion of Christ is love, of spreading love everywhere you go: first of all in your own home, maybe your children, maybe your wife or husband, maybe a next-door neighbour, love begins at home.

Our Sisters are working now in many countries, facing many difficulties because of the people who are suffering so much, but there is something very beautiful in our poor people, they are so eager, they are so lovable, they are so

56

delicate in their love, we have to know them, and we can know them only if we go to them.

Very often I ask people to come to our home for the dying — we have a big place in Calcutta and in the twenty-one years we have picked up over twenty-seven thousand people from the streets — and I ask the people not to come and to give things, things I can get for the asking. But I want their presence just to touch them, just to smile on them, just to be present there — it means such a lot to our people : some time for our lepers, for our crippled, for our unloved, uncared for children, it is the same need. They need love, that compassion, that touch, as the priest touches the Host during Mass and he touches of the body of Christ on the altar — it is that touch, with that love, with that faith, we have to touch the body of Christ in the poor. It is the same Jesus who meets Saul on the way to Damascus, who was on his way to disturb, to kill, to destroy the Christians, and He asks, 'Saul, Saul why dost thou persecute Me?' And Saul asks, 'Who are thou Lord?' 'I am Jesus Christ thou persecutest.'

And today it is the same cry, the same cry, the same Jesus, the same today in our poor people who are unwanted, unemployed, uncared for, hungry and naked and homeless. They are useless, so to say, to society and nobody has time for them, and it is you and I as Christians, burdened with that love of Christ if our love is true, we must find them, we must help them, we must bring them to Him. They are there for the finding and here in this city, great city of London, there is so much, so much that you and I can do. The first time I was here in London and we went out at night it was a terrible cold night and I found the people on the street. And there was an old man, a well-spoken man, shivering with cold. And this gentleman would say, 'Take me, take me anywhere. I am longing to sleep between two sheets.' He was a well-spoken man, he must have had better days and yet there he was.

And if we look round we will see many, not as many as in

Calcutta, not as many maybe as in other places, but here there are many. Even if it is one, he is Jesus, he is the one that is hungry for love, for care, and as it is written in the scripture, 'I looked for one to care for me and I didn't find one.' How terrible it would be if Jesus had to say that to us today, after dying for us on the cross.

SELECTED BIBLIOGRAPHY

Something Beautiful for God, Malcolm Muggeridge. Collins, London.

Mother Teresa, Desmond Doig. Collins, London. Veritas, Dublin.

chapter six

BROTHER ROGER 1974

The village of Taizé is perched on a hill near the world-renowned monastic settlement of medieval times — Cluny. The village itself is typically French and peasant-like, but there similarities end, for to this place in the 1940's came a Swiss Protestant of French-Swiss parentage and there began a movement at first associated with helping people escape Nazi persecution. After the end of World War II Roger Schutz founded the Community of Taizé which in recent years has both Catholics and Protestants within its membership.

On my first visit there, just before Easter 1974, some twenty thousand young people were sleeping out on the mist-covered hillside in tents. They, like many thousands before them and indeed after them, had come to join in a period of meditation, reflection and listening. Brother Roger, the Prior of the Taizé Community, was awarded the 1974 Prize because he has done more than anyone else to revitalize religion among young people of Europe.

In today's world Taizé is a contradiction. There is none of the rat-race atmosphere, there is none of the turbulence of violence, there is a quest not just for otherworldliness but how to have that authentic spiritual ring in a contemporary society. The community at Taizé has submitted itself to a common rule, a common impulse stimulates the community discipline which is so essential for the life of a Christian. Architects, printers, theologians, lawyers, have submitted themselves to this discipline and the impact of such not only on the commonly called Christian world, but in other major religions of the world, has been phenomenal.

This was seen particularly on Easter Day 1973 when some eighteen thousand young people were at Taizé to hear Brother Roger give more details about the opening of the worldwide Council of Youth. He called for a great mobility of young people on several continents which led to the great Council of Youths taking place in August 1974 and in the following months in Africa, Latin America, Asia and North America. Their one desire was to seek without fear of the unknown, to explore simultaneously all the dimensions of the people of God, moving their doubt towards belief; seeking to inscribe the gospel within the history of man and revealing to one another the creative capacities hidden within each one.

Since its inception Taizé has been the centre of a tireless seeking after communion, one that unites Christians first and foremost with those who are oppressed and with the God who reveals himself. When the judges had decided on Brother Roger and I phoned to talk about the award, alas he was not there — like Mother Teresa the year before. The man who had inspired thousands of young people to meditate and think of things spiritual was himself in seclusion in a Spanish hillside chalet doing exactly that. Three days later a note was passed to him and we talked to each other by telephone, largely due to international co-operation between telephone operators in London, Paris and Madrid. Roger, while accepting the award, was conscious of the rules of his community and wanted to discuss it further with the brothers. He let me know that Holy

60

Week — the time when the award was to be presented — was indeed one of the busiest weeks at the community, but following consultation with his brothers he came to London. That journey itself was an organization man's nightmare. With the major airports in France and Britain closed by fog, one was neither certain nor sure, but could only hope, that Air France might just arrive — and they did.

The presentation that year was made by Prince Philip at Windsor Castle in a room where kings and queens and members of the Most Noble Order of the Garter had been before. Lord Thurlow spoke of the work Brother Roger had done and was doing and Prince Philip, speaking in French, said how important work among young people was as he himself is patron of an award for young people in Britain.

Brother Roger, in accepting the award that year, made it known that he would not keep the money, which by then was £40,000, but rather at the suggestion of young people then at Taizé it would go to help pave the way for reconciliation among young Protestants and Catholics in Northern Ireland, among Pakistani immigrant young people in Britain, and among similar youth groups in Africa.

In the programme for the public ceremony at Guildhall, when the chair was taken by the Earl of March and Kinrara, a leading Anglican layman and chairman of CORAT—a group of professional men dedicated to helping churches in managerial and organizational work — the following was said: 'When Brother Roger first arrived in Taizé, he was quite alone. It was in 1940 that he came to the small village, near Cluny, searching for a place to begin a community. His choice fell on Taizé because of its location, in an area torn by war, for the demarcation line between free and occupied France ran just north of the village. Acquiring a house, he lived a daily prayer, later to become that of the brothers, and used his home to receive refugees, especially Jews escaping from the Nazi occupation. At the end of the war, the brothers obtained permission to receive German prisoners from a camp in the region.

'On Easter Sunday, 1949, the first brothers undertook life commitments to celibacy, community of Good and the acceptance of an authority. "The Lord Christ, in his mercy and his love for you, has chosen you to be a sign of brotherly love within the Church. He wills that with your brothers you should realize the parable of the community."

'The brothers are seeking to live a parable of communion between Christians, to end the scandal of centuries of division. The brothers belong to many different denominations, including, with the agreement of the Archbishop of Paris, Roman Catholics. They come from different countries in Europe, as well as North and South America and Africa. Through their prayer, their work and deflection, they are attempting to bring about a unity between Christians that is visible. As a community, Taizé therefore does not belong to any denomination.

'But the Church is not an end in itself. It exists for mankind. The single aim of a visible communion between Christians is to make the Church more credible; that the Church becomes a place of communion, open to all men, where everyone can feel at ease, yet without constraint to adhere to the faith of Christians.

'From the very beginning, the community has been involved in development. In the immediate region, different co-operative projects have been set up, and when the number of brothers reached twelve, several were sent to work in the neighbouring mining area. Further afield, small groups of brothers live for periods of fraternities among the poor. Presently there are brothers in Brazil, in Niger and in India.

'Wherever they are, the brothers' lives are centred on prayer, meeting together for prayer three times a day. They earn their livelihood by their work, and never accept gifts for themselves.

'For the first twenty years of its life, the community re-
mained relatively isolated. Gradually, young people started
going each year in increasing numbers. After several years
of welcoming youth from many countries, there came the
idea of a worldwide "Council of Youth". The preparation
for the Council was announced by Brother Roger at Easter
1970. Throughout the world, many thousands of young
people are now involved in it, through meetings in Taizé,
or on other continents, and by involvement in their local
situations. The search for awareness, for justice and for a
new spiritual dimension is stimulated by exchanges and
visits by small international teams of young people travelling from country to country. The Council will open at
Taizé on 30th August, 1974. Thereafter, similar opening
meetings will be held on each continent.'
The speeches of the Earl of March and Mr John Templeton,
the founder of the award, referred to the way in which
Brother's Roger's work had clearly led to a deeper understanding of God by many young people. 'Brother Roger
and the community of Taizé have over the past years given
to the world a new vision of the creativity of God.'
In awarding the Prize to Brother Roger the Foundation in
its citation spoke of his 'being instrumental in widening
or deepening man's knowledge and love of God through
his worldwide work among young people and his efforts
for renewal and reconciliation and thereby furthering the
quest for the quality of life that mirrors the Divine.'

Address of the Earl of March and Kinrara

I feel greatly humbled that I should have been invited to
chair this ceremony today, but I am not at all sure why I
have been. Perhaps it is because I am British and involved
in the life of the Churches in this country and because the
ceremony is being held in Britain. That enables me to say
to Mr Templeton on behalf of all of us who are British
here today how honoured we are that he should have
decided that this country would be the location for the

presentation of his Foundation's prize; for it gives us the opportunity to meet in the flesh and to offer our respect to a few of those persons from other countries, and to other Churches and other religions who by their life and work give real meaning to that increasingly overworked phrase 'improving the quality of life' and, to quote the objective of the Templeton Prize, who 'stimulate the knowledge and love of God on that part of mankind everywhere'. For me, personally, the presentation of this Prize here today most particularly emphasizes the increasing interdependence of all men and, therefore, the need for greater concern by all men and women for all other men and women everywhere in the world of whatever nation, race, age, wealth or creed.

The judges, men and women, come from different nations, races and religions. The Prize itself has been given last year to Mother Teresa, a Christian woman, member of the Roman Catholic Church, working among the poor people in a country where Christians are in a minority. This year the Prize goes to Brother Roger, a Christian man, member of the Protestant Church, working especially among young people of all Churches and none, in a country where his own Church is in a small minority. The policy of the judges is clearly ecumenical in the widest meaning of the word — universal.

Personally, I am delighted that it should be so, because it lends weight to the growing importance for all men everywhere of what in the Churches we call the Ecumenical Movement to which I am deeply committed through my membership of the World Council of Churches as a representative of the Church of England.

Unfortunately the only aspect of the World Council's work of which most people in this country hear anything is the policy of making grants to certain organizations of oppressed people round the world through the programme to combat racism. But the World Council of Churches stands for much more and does much more than just that one programme. It carries out in the name of Christ and of all the member Churches a massive relief operation to refugees and poor people throughout the world; it concerns itself with the cry of the oppressed round the world for social justice; it has started to do something about the need for development in the so-called Third World; it brings together bishops, priests and lay people, academics, pastors and administrators to discuss and act on matters of the doctrine, worship, witness and mission of the Churches; it brings together in dialogue the representatives of all religions and of ideologies and of none; it gathers together representatives of all the Christian Churches in the further-ance of the unity of the Church throughout the world.

It is the one institution in the world in which people from all over the world come together to discuss their common problems and opportunities not simply on the basis of their common humanity, as in the United Nations, but also on a commonly held fundamental conviction, namely confession that the Lord Jesus Christ is Saviour according to the Scriptures. It is not surprising that some of its state-ments and actions should be unpopular in one part of the world or another; the more it becomes a genuinely world body that will more and more likely be so; for the objective of the Christian Church should not be the avoidance of controversy or a striving after popularity but a deep commitment to God's truth through our Lord Jesus Christ.

Address of Mr John M. Templeton

Mr Templeton emphasized that the Templeton Prize is intended to bring much greater benefit to others than to the recipient in order that they may gain a better under-standing of the infinity of God. He said he hoped to inspire more young people to devote their lives to being useful tools in God's hands and clear channels through which his love can flow. He again emphasized that the Templeton Prize is not merely a prize for religion, it is a prize for progress.

I would go to the ends of the earth, I would go right round the world, to tell and tell again of my trust in the new generation, my confidence in youth.

And it is for us, the older generation, to listen, never to condemn. Listen and again listen, to grasp what is finest in the creative intuition that dwells within the young today.

They will trace our paths, they will overcome barriers, they will open breaches, to carry the whole people of God along with them. Above all, they will know how to get beyond the demarcation lines that separate believers from one another or that separate believer from non-believer.

For me, right from my own youth, I have had the conviction that being a man, having a heart filled with humanity, means never condemning but above all understanding everything of other people.

The young can be judged by certain older people in a way that brooks no appeal, and there are young people whose attitude to the older generation is one of rejection. This generation gap is quite contrary to the sense of the universal. Both risk losing much by it: the young, because they are depriving themselves of human and spiritual experience, the old, because they are relegating themselves to a situation where they passively await their own death. And yet life is a gift of God, for the old as for the young.

When we listen to the young, with the left ear and with the right, which means, when we take them such as they are, we discover an immense diversity of aspirations, a vast plurality.

This is what I have been discovering over the last four years, through the preparation for the Worldwide Council of Youth which will open soon on the different continents. As I think of the Council of Youth, I cannot bring myself to worry, even when people put their finger on the great difficulties and the tensions that we must face. I have such confidence in the intuitions of the young from so many countries, who are gathering at Taizé, who come, who go off again, who search, who pray.

Struggle and Contemplation

Recapitulating their aspirations, there are two intuitions that emerge: struggle and contemplation.

Struggle, which struggle do we mean? A struggle for the liberation of all men, to give a voice to the man who has no voice, to promote a society without classes, a lifelong commitment alongside the man who is victim of man. Many young people have understood that communion with the misery of the world is also participation in the world's struggle against misery. And the thick of this struggle, in the rich countries as in the poor, the believer's place is not in the rearguard. They are called to expose themselves in order to take risks.

Yet the struggle for and with man finds its source in yet another struggle, a struggle inscribed at the very heart of our being, there where no man resembles any other. There we touch the very doors of contemplation.

Contemplation is nothing other than one's whole person being seized by the reality of the love of God. When we understand a truth of the natural order with our minds, we can be seized by it, but only partially. On the contrary in contemplation, it is in the depths of our being that we are seized by the unique reality, the reality of the love of God, which fills even the emptiness which each man knows deep within himself.

Here, it is love that is the touchstone. Discovering a face to face meeting with God . . . contemplating him too in the face of man . . . and giving back a human face to the man who is disfigured. All this is one and the same struggle — that of love. To the point that nothing is grave except the loss of love.

In many of the young, the marked sense of being part of a worldwide human community allows us to discern a fairly new consciousness of the universal. For Christians, this openness to the universal supposes a definite communion among themselves, whereas they have been so divided through the centuries. First of all finding unity in one's own person, being reconciled in oneself, so as to be led toward reconciliation with others. Not so as to be more powerful, in a crusading spirit, but to be men of reconciliation and to offer a place of communion to all men. For Christians, this place of communion is the body of Christ, the place that is called the Church. A great number of young people reject the Church, unless it becomes a place of communion where even the unbeliever can feel himself at ease, yet without his being asked to adhere to it; unless too it becomes a place of communion without means of power, free from links with powers that be and compromise with financial power. Through history, Christians have retreated so far from the community of goods that was a fact in the life of the early Church. Poverty of means helps us to be men of communion, it will always be linked to the creation of a universal communion.

Communion of Love

To support a communion of love among all men, I myself have great hope in all that comes to us from the Southern hemisphere. And this hope finds itself confirmed through so many young people from the southern continents that I meet constantly and with whom we are searching.

This hope even marked my childhood. My parents foresaw a decline in faith within Europe. As a child, I heard my father and mother express their firm confidence that a renewal of faith would come to us through African Christians. In essence, they said: It is the African Christians who will bring the Gospel in its first freshness to people in the Northern hemisphere. They even arranged for their nine children (myself, the youngest) to hear a personal word from an elderly African, a man of God, who was travelling in Europe.

This meeting with the African marked my life and continues to quicken me from within. It has been a determining factor in the high expectation I have had ever since towards the men of the southern continents, South American, African, Asian.

Now let me say something about the Templeton Prize. I did not expect to receive it. When I heard about it, I thought of Mother Teresa who received it last year, and of my own brothers of Taizé who are working with Mother Teresa this year, among the dying in Calcutta.

Then I said to myself: 'You have always refused honours and distinctions. Receive the Templeton Prize with simplicity of heart, uniquely as a confirmation of Buddhist, Hindu, Muslim, Jewish and Christian believers, addressed to the believer that you, day after day, are seeking to be.'

As for the sum of money which goes with the Prize, I do not accept it for the Taizé community. We have always refused gifts. We have always lived entirely from our work, without any capital in reserve. Again, I cannot accept it for the reception of the tens of thousands of young people who come to Taizé, even although at this moment the reception fund is empty.

Money to whom?

Over the past weeks, I have been able to ask large numbers of young people staying with us on the hill, as to whom the money from the Templeton Prize should be given. It will be given to poor young people, especially in the Southern hemisphere who, committed in the ways of struggle and contemplation are seeking to meet one another and to be tireless seekers of communion. A first sum of money will be left here in the British Isles, for young people working among immigrants from Africa and Asia, especially Pakistanis, and also for young people struggling for reconciliation in Northern Ireland.

To conclude, let me express to you my hope in what lies before us: a springtime is at hand, soon it will warm us

69

with the ardour of its fire. One of the stakes is our communion, between youth and older people.

Certain evenings I happen to be out walking alone, under
a sky heavy with stars. Thousands of young people are
staying on the hill. I can hear them in the distance and I
say for myself; the multitude of intuitions of these young
people glimmer like streaks of fire in my night. For the
present, there is nothing that can be readily perceived,
and yet my night is festival, it is ablaze, it is filled with
unfathomable hope. And I repeat to myself: nothing is
grave except the loss of love.

SELECTED BIBLIOGRAPHY

Festival, Brother Roger. Taizé Press.
The Rule of Taizé, Brother Roger. Taizé Press.
Dare to Live, Brother Roger, SPCK, London.

chapter seven

DR SARVEPALLI RADHAKRISHNAN
1975

Dr Sarvepalli Radhakrishnan is perhaps more widely known as a President of India but in the world of philosophy and religious thought he made his outstanding contribution as Spalding Professor of Eastern Religions and Ethics at the University of Oxford in England. One modern writer has said of him: 'He achieved far more than the presidency of India, not since Ficht and Schelling has there been such a precipitate stream of inspiration. Except for an occasional Marcus Aurelius, philosophers will never be kings. Sometimes, however, a philosopher wields an influence that a king might covet. Such an influence is wielded by Dr Radhakrishnan. For to mediate creatively between the Indian heritage and her meaningful present is to pour grave responsibilities before the whole world.'

It was this king of modern philosophy who was not a philosopher of the East or of the West but rather a bridge of understanding between the cultures and religions of the hemispheres. In coming to their conclusion, the judges decided that Dr Radhakrishnan 'led the rediscovery of the understanding of God and his special contribution to modern Hinduism is one of the most outstanding features in world religion today' and so awarded him the 1974 Prize.

Unfortunately, age at this time had a telling effect and when the Prize was to be presented Dr Radhakrishnan was too ill to attend. He died within two weeks. Before his death he asked that the monetary part of the award be used to set up a fellowship at Oxford for postgraduate studies and research work by Indian students who wish to further probe his life and thought.

Mr K. D. D. Henderson, writing in the programme for the public ceremony at Guildhall said: 'It is difficult to summarize the career of a man who was Professor of Philosophy at three successive universities in India, and held the Spalding Chair of Eastern Religions and Ethics at Oxford for sixteen years; who was three times a Vice Chancellor; Indian Ambassador in Moscow from 1949 to 1952; Vice-President of India from 1952 to 1962; and President of India from 1962 to 1967.

'As a philosopher-ruler he came nearer to Plato's dream than anyone since Asoka. As a combination of philosopher, statesman and religious reformer he is unique.

'From the time of the publication, in 1920, of his first book, *The Reign of Religion in Contemporary Philosophy*, Radhakrishnan has made a greater contribution than any other of his distingusihed generation to the cross-fertilization of ideas between religion and philosophy and between eastern and western thought.

'He was equally at home in both the ideological worlds in which he sojourned and in the third world in which he was born; but he had his being in a fourth world, a world of his own creation, above all these. He did not transcend boundaries; he abolished them; so that dialogue with him took place in a climate of opinion in which "they" had ceased to exist and "we" held varied opinions, arguing not to prove a case but to unearth a truth.

'All Souls, with its unique reputation for combining eru-

Prince Philip presents the 1975 award to The Indian High Commissioner to London Mr Nerhu for Dr Sarvepalli Radhakrishnan the recipient.

Dr Sarvepalli Radhakrishnan, the recipient for 1975.

dition with practical politics, was not ill-suited to his special genius, and it was to All Souls that he loved to come when visiting this country in his later years.

'But for all his diplomatic and academic triumphs it is in the field of religious understanding that his name will chiefly be remembered. Tolerance was defined by his friend Richard Livingstone as a mean between intolerance and indifference. It is too often associated with the latter. This was never true of Sarvepalli Radhakrishnan, and his most important role has been in that change of the climate of opinion amongst theologians and religious leaders all over the world which has been such a feature of the last quarter century. Muslim and Hindu still eye one another askance in his own beloved sub-continent; Muslim and Jew across Jordan; Catholic and Protestant in Ulster; communist and theist across the Iron Curtain. But all these differences are political more than religious or philosophical. Up at the top, in the world of theology and ideology, the *rapprochement*, and the growing mutual understanding and respect, are there for all to see. They will filter down.

'In the progress to this position it might be said that Radhakrishnan has done more than any other man to put across the Hindu point of view, just as Dr Suzuki did more than any other man to put across the idea of Zen Buddhism as he saw it. But Radhakrishnan did not put across the Hindu viewpoint; he infused it. Raymond Panikkar wrote of the unknown Christ in Hinduism. Radhakrishnan made men aware of the unknown Hinduism in the teaching of Christ, a truth reflected in the legend that Jesus visited India and studied the Sanskrit and Pali texts. As Robin Zaehner, Radhakrishnan's successor in the Spalding Chair pointed out, there is a certain incongruity between the Yahweh of the Old Testament chroniclers and the God of the New.

'If one has to find an example of the breadth of Radhakrishnan's outlook in the world of ideas and ideologies, one might do worse than quote his reply to the debate, at

Francis Younghusband's famous first World Congress of Faiths in 1936, which followed his paper on Religion and Religions.

' "The Question has been raised," he said, "that those who believed in intuition used to exclude the operation of the intellect." The way the leader of the debate put it was that those who practise do not investigate, and those who investigate do not practise. But if you go to the really great mystics, whether in the Upanishads, or to a man like the Buddha, or one like Plato, or any of the great mystics of the world who may be regarded as examples of saintly life, you will find in them an intellectual eminence and comprehensive knowledge. And it would have been impossible for them to practise those things unless their intellects had been satisfied. The life of the spirit is an integral life, a life where you sanctify your body, illuminate your intellect, and obtain a complete kind of manhood. There should, in any complete life, be equal emphasis on the intellect and the intuitions.'

Diplomats from many countries mingled in Guildhall with religious leaders and members of congregations for the public ceremony of the award to this remarkable man who has led to the rediscovery of the understanding of God and made a special contribution to modern Hinduism. These are two of the outstanding features in world religion today. The award was received on behalf of Dr Radhakrishnan by India's High Commissioner to London, Shri B. K. Nehru, who in his speech said: 'Dr Radhakrishnan, one of the most religious men of this century, religion is universal and recognizes neither national boundaries nor differences in forms of belief. Religion, he says, is "neither unworldly nor other-worldly . . . neither a creed nor a code, but an insight into reality". Men, he points out, are "asking for reality in religion; they want to penetrate to the depths of life, tear away the veils that hide the primordial reality and learn what is essential for life, for truth, and righteousness." Religion is not "an apologetic for the existing social

order; nor is it a mere instruction for social salvation. . . .
It is an attempt to discover the ideal possibilities of human
life, a quest for emancipation from the immediate compulsions of vain and petty moods." Religion is "essentially
a concern of the inner life. Its roots lie in the spirit of man,
deeper than feeling, will or intellect. . . . Its end is to
secure spiritual certainty which lifts life above meaningless
existence or dull despair," to raise us "from our momentary meaningless provincialism to the significance and
status of the eternal, to transform the chaos and confusion
of life."

'Religion to him "is not a refuge from the world but an
inspiration to act in the world." It is "an inspiration to
grow into the likeness of the Divine," because "the Divine
is both in us and out of us," and "the Divine in us is the
source of perfection of nature." Because truth to him is
not the exclusive possession of any one individual, class,
race or religion, Dr Radhakrishnan in his search for it went
far beyond the confines of his country to explore the spirit
and fountainheads of Truth. It was to him a never-ending,
life-long search and this is what he has discovered, "God
does not say, I am Tradition, but he says, I am Truth. Truth
is greater than its greatest teachers." He found support
and comfort from those words of Ghandi, "The quest for
truth is the *summum bonum* of life." '

The Archbishop of Canterbury, The Most Reverend Dr
Donald Coggan, who chaired that ceremony said : 'His
ethical judgements and his political judgements sprang —
have always sprung — from a deep religious interpretation
of the universe, and I think it would be true to say that
his two most honoured and revered friends were Rabindranath Tagore and Ghandi — that is a very significant
couple of friendships in their influence on this great world
citizen. He is well versed in our own Biblical literature
and has a wide knowledge of Christian theology as well as
a deep understanding of the whole tradition of India.'

In a private ceremony at Buckingham Palace, Prince Philip

recalled the first time he met Dr Radhakrishnan who, though in a position of supreme importance in his country, was a humble man with a fertile mind whose thoughts were always for a better understanding of his fellow man and of his creator.

Address by the Archbishop of Canterbury

This is the third occasion on which we have met in connexion with this Templeton Foundation. It is almost unnecessary for me to say how great is the debt that we owe to Mr Templeton from whom we shall be hearing later in the proceedings, but without his generosity this wonderful Foundation would never have come to pass, nor would these generous awards have been made. It is only right, I think, that at the beginning of our meeting today I should pay this tribute to him and to his wife, whom we are delighted to see here today.

We meet in connexion with the award to a very great man. Only once have I had the privilege of converse with him and that was a good many years ago in New Delhi, but the impression made is not easily forgotten. I do not think it is my task this afternoon to give anything like a resume of his life, nor if I were able to do so, of his very extensive and learned writings. But there can be no doubt that in making this award it is being made to a citizen of world stature.

It cannot, I think, be said of many that they have an intimate and detailed knowledge of four great cultural traditions, but this can certainly be said of Dr Radhakrishnan. He knows his United States, for he has very frequently travelled and lectured there; he knows his Britain, because for many years he was professor at Oxford — he gave the Upton Lectures in 1926, the Hibbert Lectures in 1929, and the Spalding Lectures a decade later, and he was one of those very few people to whom the high and distinguished award of the Order of Merit was given. He knows his Russia, for he was the Ambassador of his country to that country; and he knows, needless to say, few better, his own native country of India, and as I learnt this morning, bears as his first name the name of the village from which he sprang.

He was, as we all know, Vice-President of that great nation for a decade, and President for another. That is by any reckoning a very distinguished record. When he served his nation as Vice-President and President he did it as far more than a political figurehead. He was deeply concerned, as all his speeches show, with the relations of India with the rest of the world, and during the sad conflict in 1965 between India and Pakistan, there was no element of rancour to his utterances, but throughout he stood, as he did indeed in all his political career, for honesty and for truth. His ethical judgements and his political judgements sprang — have always sprung — from a deep religious interpretation of the universe, and I think it would be true to say that his two most honoured and revered friends were Rabindranath Tagore and Ghandi — that is a very significant couple of friendships in their influence on this great world citizen. He is well versed in our own Biblical literature and has a wide knowledge of Christian theology as well as a deep understanding of the whole tradition of India.

Anthony Eden tells how on one occasion he was visiting India and had the privilege of addressing a session of the Houses of Parliament there. But he found his task a somewhat intimidating one, for he had to follow Radhakrishnan, who introduced him to his audience. Anthony Eden expresses his feelings in these words: 'I felt like a little boy stumbling across a ploughed field after a leveret had shown its swiftly light paces.'

That is a very fair suggestion as to the greatness not only in speech but also in thought of him who is today being honoured with this third award of the Templeton Foundation.

Your Grace, Your Excellencies, Ladies and Gentlemen, to-day we meet for the third presentation of the Templeton Foundation Prize for Progress in Religion. And today we are pleased to honour one of the greatest thinkers of the Hindu faith.

In his earlier years, Dr Rahdakrishnan was a man far ahead of his time; but today philosophers and theologians of most faiths acknowledge his greatness and the break-throughs he has made in the twentieth century.

Dr Radhakrishnan has been described by the Public Orator at Oxford as 'The philosopher-king of whom Plato dream-ed'. But he is more than even that. He is one of the inspired men who has helped to rediscover the meanings of life on earth. To Radhakrishnan, his relationship with the Eternal is of prime importance. This rediscovery may be his greatest contribution to modern Hinduism and to the other religions of the world. Each of us can grow in our personal faiths by being more God centred. Indeed, one could say of Dr Radhakrishnan that his catholicity is unexcelled.

Because of our birth, culture, history and race, we will view God in different ways. But surely we can learn from each other. By studying other people's ideas, we may understand better the wonders of God's creation, his mean-ing for history and the future of mankind. Indeed, by sharing together the rich variety of visions we may, in the end, better understand each other. Each of us is inspired spiritually when we hear about the dedicated souls in each religion who have found new ways to increase man's love of God and man's surrender to the infinite spirit.

All of us worship the same creator, the same ground of being, the same supreme spirit which is infinite, omni-present and omniscient. Each of us worships in a different way, because we understand so little. The purpose of life on earth may be for each man to grow more spiritually and in the love and understanding of God.

It is arrogant of atheists to say there is no God because

even the best scientists can perceive only a tiny fraction of what exists in the universe. Throughout history religion has often led to wars, inquisitions and martyrdom, but only because man was not humble about how little he understood about an infinite God.

Nations have gone to war to force upon others their own idea of God. This could not happen if each of us worships God in humility, admitting that no man and no church will ever understand even one per cent of God. God is infinite and we are limited in our knowledge. We may learn more if we approach God in humility, not thinking we know it all. I believe that God is all of us and each of us is a little part of Him. Each of the millions of galaxies is a little part of the infinite Creator. Each of us may be in reality only a wave pattern, a symphony in the mind of the infinite Creator. In the infinite spirit we live and move and have our being. The greater part of our Creator is the unseen part. When any man says he knows all about God, he has pictured in his human mind a god so small that he is no god at all.

Humility causes an open mind, which in turn makes it possible for us to learn from each other. An open mind causes progress. One of the purposes of our Prize Programme is to cause humility by helping people of all nations to learn about the rich variety of ways that other men love and understand the Supreme Spirit. Also, competition causes progress. It may be good for the great visions and revelations to compete with each other in a loving neighbourly way. If the earth knew only one religion, mankind's spiritual progress would be slow. When scientists study the history of the millions of types of life on earth, many conclude that the Creator has ordained competition for the purpose of progress.

It is this progress we seek. It is this wider understanding of God we pursue; and it is this enrichment by cultural and spiritual diversity that may enable mankind to move forward to a future called heaven on earth.

In conclusion, we are grateful to each of the nine judges who have been diligent in their consideration of the nominees and to the Board of Advisors who work to improve this programme. We are grateful to His Grace the Archbishop of Canterbury for presiding here this afternoon. And we are grateful to His Royal Highness Prince Philip for presenting the third annual Prize for Progress in Religion to Dr Radhakrishnan's representative today at Buckingham Palace.

After this celebration you are welcome to join us for tea in the crypt below where you will have an opportunity to meet the judges and others on this platform.

Address by Shri B. K. Nehru, High Commissioner for India

I am happy and honoured, in spite of my own unworthiness, to accept the Templeton Prize on behalf of Dr Radhakrishnan. He is unfortunately prevented by a serious illness from receiving it personally. He has expressed his wish that the money that goes with the Prize should be used in a teaching institution for the furtherance of his work and discussions on this have already been initiated by members of his family. But I should like, before going any further, to thank Mr Templeton and the Templeton Foundation for having instituted the Prize, the Members of the Jury for awarding this year's Prize to Dr Radhakrishnan and His Royal Highness the Duke of Edinburgh for presenting the Prize to me on behalf of Dr Radhakrishnan this morning at Buckingham Palace.

World religion is richer today, as the citation of the Award says, because of Dr Radhakrishnan's re-discovery of the understanding of God and his special contribution to modern Hinduism. To this may I add my personal tribute that by promoting mutual understanding between the philosophies of the East and West, Dr Radhakrishnan has rendered inestimable service to the world.

There are few scholars like him who are erudite in both Indian and Western philosophy. Few thinkers are there like him who could grasp the spirit of Eastern and Western thought alike and speak to the East and to the West in a language that each can understand. A philosopher-linguist and a liaison officer between two civilizations, as he has been described, Dr Radhakrishnan has acted as the bridge between the Orient and the Occident, expounding to the Western world the philosophy and religion of India — a country which has been historically the meeting ground of various races, cultures and faiths and given half of the world's population much of its religious education.

To Dr Radhakrishnan, one of the most religious men of this century, religion is universal and recognizes neither national boundaries nor differences in forms of belief. Religion, he says, is 'neither unworldly nor other-worldly . . . neither a creed nor a code, but an insight into reality'. Men, he points out, are 'asking for reality in religion; they want to penetrate to the depths of life, tear away the veils that hide the primordial reality and learn what is essential for life, for truth, and righteousness.' Religion is not 'an apologetic for the existing social order; nor is it a mere instruction for social salvation. . . . It is an attempt to discover the ideal possibilities of human life, a quest for emancipation from the immediate compulsions of vain and petty moods.' Religion is 'essentially a concern of the inner life. Its roots lie in the spirit of man, deeper than feeling, will or intellect. . . . Its end is to secure spiritual certainty which lifts life above meaningless existence or dull despair,' to raise us 'from our momentary meaningless provincialism to the significance and status of the eternal, to transform the chaos and confusion of life.'

Religion to him 'is not a refuge from the world but an inspiration to act in the world.' It is 'an inspiration to grow into the likeness of the Divine,' because 'the Divine is both in us and out of us,' and 'the Divine in us is the source of perfection of nature.' Because truth is not the exclusive possession of any one individual, class, race or religion, Dr Radhakrishnan in his search for it went far beyond the confines of his country to explore the spirit and fountain-heads of Truth. It was to him a never-ending, life-long search and this is what he has discovered. 'God does not say, I am Tradition, but he says, I am Truth. Truth is greater than its greatest teachers.' He found support and comfort from those words of Ghandi, 'The quest for truth is the *summum bonum* of life.'

Time and again, in his writings and speeches, Dr Radhakrishnan has emphasized today's needs for 'the union of hearts, the communion of minds,' and for 'multi-cultural understanding and spiritual fellowship,' if our social, economic, cultural and political institutions are to be saved. We have, he once says, the resources of 'science and technology by which we can feed the whole world' and transmit and communicate ideas all over the world. 'All that is necessary is a shake-up of human nature, regeneration of human nature.' To him the 'achievements of knowledge and power are not enough; acts of spirit and morality are essential.' 'We must build all relationships on a basis of understanding fellowship, remembering the controlling principle that life on each is meaningless apart from its eternal background' and that 'only a humanity that strives after ethical and spiritual ideals can use the great triumphs of scientific knowledge for the true end of civilization.'

If Dr Radhakrishnan has a vision of a new world, it is a world built by people 'who have deepened their personalities and integrated their lives; people who have 'direct acquaintance with spiritual reality'; people who 'attain their deepest self by losing their selfish ego'; people who can lift their own spirit 'from the thraldom of material things'; people for whom 'every morning brings a new day and every pulse beat a new life.'

I wonder what thoughts haunt Dr Radhakrishnan these days and months as he lies on his sick bed. Would he murmur to himself these words of St Paul: 'I have fought a good fight. I have run the race'? Or would his soul ring out with this prayer from the *Upanishads*:

Asato Ma Sadgamaya
Tamaso Ma Jyotirgamaya
Mrityorma Amritam Gamaya
Om Shantih Shantih Shantih

(Lead me from the unreal to the real,
Lead me from darkness to light,
Lead me from death to eternal life)

If Dr Radhakrishnan has any message for us this afternoon, he would probably choose the closing lines of his book *My Search for Truth*. May I read them to you?
'Truly religious souls from Buddha and Christ down to lesser mortals, in spite of gross defects of nature, of mind and heart, have striven to lighten the loads of humanity, to strengthen the hopes without which it would have fainted and fallen in its difficult journey. If we are to imitate in some small measure their example, we must help the weak and comfort the unhappy. The perception that casts a shadow over one's existence is that one is not able to take a larger share of the burden of pain that lies upon the world, with its poor and lowly, with its meek and suffering. It does not matter if one has to live one's days in silence, if only it is given to them to smile at a child sometimes, to comfort another human soul in a way that will cheer him and put new hope into his heart.'

SELECTED BIBLIOGRAPHY
Radhakrishnan, R. P. Singh. Stirling Publications, Delhi.

chapter eight

CARDINAL SUENENS 1976

When the Templeton Prize was first presented a number of people said that following the choice of Mother Teresa it would be difficult in future years to award the Prize to people of her calibre. During the winter months of 1975 the judges had indeed a difficult task but for another reason in that a number of candidates for the award had made such outstanding contributions to world religion in our time. However, they concluded that Cardinal Suenens was the most outstanding of those names before them.

When I telephoned Cardinal Suenens at his residence in Malines his secretary, Canon Brieven, said the Cardinal was holding his weekly diocesan meeting. I intimated to the Canon why I was calling and when I later that day spoke to the Cardinal he replied: 'It is of the Lord.'

This phrase is so typical of the Cardinal. He was born in Brussels on 16th July 1904, the son of a restaurateur. The boy was only three-and-a-half when his father died. He received his early education in Brussels, firstly at the school of the Marist Brothers, later at the Institut Sainte-Marie which was run by diocesan priests. He graduated first in his class and on being called to the priesthood was sent by Cardinal Mercier to Rome where he studied philosophy and theology at the Gregorian University. He received the Doctorates in Philosophy and Theology and a Baccalaureate in Canon Law. Throughout this period he kept up an intimate correspondence with Cardinal Mercier who had a profound influence upon the young Suenens.

He was ordained priest in Rome on 4th September 1927 and continued his studies there until 1929. He then became for a short period a teacher at the Institut Sainte-Marie in Brussels. At the end of this period he became Professor of Philosophy at the Seminary of Malines for ten years. While there he taught history of philosophy and pedagogy. In this way he was not only able to have an important influence on the lives of many future priests, but also to become fully grounded in his own ecclesiastical studies.

At the beginning of the war, 1940, he was appointed Vice-Rector of the University of Louvain. The Rector was imprisoned by the Germans quite soon afterwards and Suenens therefore took on the various responsibilities of that post. While Vice-Rector he initiated the Institut des Sciences Religieuses at Louvain. He shared the view that the religious education of the laity was not given sufficient attention at university level.

On 16th December 1945 he became Auxiliary Bishop to Cardinal van Roey at Malines. He was responsible for many different aspects of diocesan life. His principal concerns were the administration of the sacraments and the censorship of books. As Cardinal van Roey grew older, Bishop Suenens took on more and more of his responsibilities. Cardinal van Roey died in 1961.

During this period Bishop Suenens discovered an apostolic organization, then little known in Belgium or indeed in Europe as a whole. This was the Legion of Mary. Realizing the great apostolic potential of the movement, he made several trips to Dublin to study the movement more closely and to hold discussions with its founder, Mr Frank Duff. As a result of this close contact Bishop Suenens wrote a commentary on the legionary's promise which appeared in book form under the title *The Theology of the Apostolate of the Legion of Mary*. He also wrote a biography of one of the movement's early and most outstanding figures, Edel Quinn.

During this same period he came into contact with the Moral Rearmament Movement — a movement which was then being discussed throughout Europe. When he became responsible for enunciating the Catholic position in relation to this movement, he spent a week at Caux in Switzerland, the centre of the movement. For many years he had close relations with the movement's directors and was invited by them to present an exposé of Catholic reservations in their regard. Finally, in order to make his position more clear to many, within and without the movement, who did not as yet understand the reasons for such reservations, he published his opinions in book form under the English title *The Right View of Moral Rearmament*.

In 1955, as Auxiliary of Malines, Bishop Suenens published a book which became the fundamental presentation of his position. All his dominant ideas concerning the pastoral mission of the Church are included. The main chapters were later developed into books in their own right.

In 1956 the school question in Belgium reached a climax. Bishop Suenens was entrusted by Cardinal van Roey with the task of negotiating with the Minister of Education in the hope of avoiding an open conflict. The result of these discussions, originally secret, later became known to the press. In any event, the conflict was not avoided and the problem was only later resolved by the *Pacte Scolaire*.

One result of these contacts was a book by Suenens *La Question Scolaire* which was an effort to both clarify the issue and calm the opposing factions.

In 1957, at the request of Daniel Rops, the editor of the *Twentieth Century Encyclopaedia*, he contributed a book, *Mary, the Mother of God*. It is a synthesis of Catholic Marian theology.

In 1959 Bishop Suenens represented Cardinal van Roey at the opening of the Catholic World Congress of Health. Addressing the three thousand members of medical and allied professions he made an appeal which has had far-reaching consequences. He asked doctors and research workers to devote their time and energy to solving the problems of birth control. It was at the same time an appeal to the universities to pursue studies into the question of human fertility so that Christians might be able to fulfil all their duties in this regard while responding fully to their dignity and obligations as Christians. This appeal resulted in a series of annual international meetings at Louvain. Three years after this appeal a new institute was created at Louvain — Institut Universitaire des Sciences Familiales et Sexologiques. Suenens also published a book under the English title of *Love and Control*.

On 15th December 1961 he was named Archbishop of Malines; and on 19th March 1962 Cardinal.

During the first few months of his administration, Cardinal Suenens divided the ancient diocese of Malines into two equal Episcopal Sees of Malines and Brussels and a third diocese of Anvers. A striking characteristic of his theory of diocesan administration was the introduction of four Archdeacons. In addition to their territorial authority they each have authority over the whole diocese in matters pertaining to their particular field. One benefit of this system is the Bishop's close contacts with local problems through the medium of the Archdeacon or Vicar-General. It is in effect a decentralization of authority and the creation of a team of Vicars-General through whom the diocese is governed.

In 1962 the Cardinal published *The Nun in the World*. This is based on a whole series of experiments, carried on by various convents, notably in Nivelles. It is a development of a chapter in *The Gospel to Every Creature*. The effect of this book throughout the world has been a great renewal of Apostolic activity on the part of women in orders.

The Cardinal's most important activity, apart from his own diocesan work, has been his work within the Second Vatican Council. Already as Auxiliary Bishop he was named a member of the Preparatory Commission to prepare the scheme on the Bishops. A few days after becoming Cardinal he was appointed a member of the Central Commission. This brought about close contacts between the Cardinal and Pope John XXIII, which were characterized by a deep mutual understanding.

The Pope was particularly impressed by the Cardinal's Pastoral Letter on the Council. He felt it reflected his own thoughts and asked the Cardinal to give written answers to certain questions, one of which was: How do you view the Council? The Cardinal's answer developed into an overall plan for the Council, according to which the Council should gravitate around the theme of the Church viewed from a double perspective: first the Church as viewed from within — that is in dialogue among its members, individually and collectively — and then as viewed from outside — in dialogue between the Church and all Christians in the world. The Pope approved this programme and alluded to it in his address of September 1962. The Council, however, opened one month later without a set plan but gradually this order became more evident and on 4th December Cardinal Suenens proposed his plan. Cardinals Montini and Lercaro endorsed this point of view.

In 1963 Pope John charged Cardinal Suenens with the responsibility of presenting the Encyclical *Pacem in Terris* to U Thant, then Secretary-General of the United Nations. This visit enabled the Cardinal to renew many friendships and to establish new and strong ties in many parts of the non-Catholic world, especially among Protestants and Orthodox.

It was also in 1963 that Pope John died. Cardinal Suenens' friend and close collaborator, Cardinal Montini, became Pope Paul VI. It was he who had written the preface to

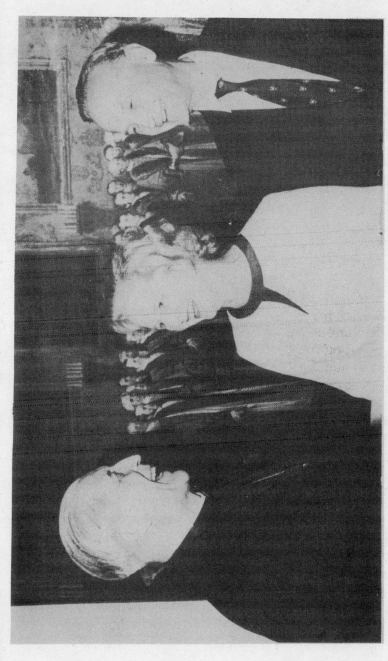

Mrs Margaret Thatcher shares a moment with Cardinal Suenens and Mr John Templeton at the 1976 ceremony in Guildhall at which Mrs Thatcher presided.

Prince Philip presents the 1976 award to Cardinal Suenens of Belgium. In the centre are Mr and Mrs John Templeton.

The Gospel to Every Creature and who had initiated the translation into Italian of *Love and Control*.

During the sessions of the Council Cardinal Suenens was named as one of the four moderators. He played a major role in the five questions which were posed to the assembly. He also made three important interventions. First to defend the idea of a permanent diaconate, in which he outlined the theological issues at stake; secondly, on the age limit of 75 for ecclesiastical superiors; thirdly, on the subject of the charisms conferred upon the laity.

The Cardinal has a continuing interest in the charismatic movement, as witness his recent publication *A New Pentecost*.

The judges in awarding the Prize to Cardinal Suenens said that he had made 'an outstanding contribution in conveying to modern man the relevance of religion in an age of confusion and doubt and he had both stimulated and promoted the need for personal renewal and reconciliation. His contribution to the reforming of the Church's structures and the prominence of the ministry of the laity have led to renewed hope and faith for many.'

There is also a new dimension in Christian circles on who the Holy Spirit is. Combined with the new thinking in relation to science and faith these make exciting reading. This was more than evident in the judges' decision to award this year the Prize to Cardinal Suenens of Belgium. Almost single-handedly he has championed within his own church the need for personal renewal and reconciliation. In his book *A New Pentecost* he not only sets sights high but has gone a long way in helping his people to attain that assurance 'that His spirit bears witness with our spirits that we are the children of God.' In his address Cardinal Suenens saw the unity of the people of God as the fruit of our spiritual renewal. As such he said : 'This visible unity reproduced powerful apostolic and political action for the service of the world.'

The renewal movement within the Christian Church greeted Cardinal Suenens' recognition as a significant step forward in recognizing the movement of the Holy Spirit in world religion today.

This was echoed by the King and Queen of the Belgians in their cable to Cardinal Suenens at Guildhall: 'We congratulate you with all our hearts for the Templeton Prize which has just been awarded to you and we rejoice with those who know of what you do for the unity of believers.'

Mrs Margaret Thatcher, leader of the British Conservative Party, who chaired the ceremony in connexion with the award said that Cardinal Suenens gave 'not only an example but a message and a sense of hope to the world,' and that the Cardinal's endeavours to 're-emphasize the potential and significance of the laity in Church affairs' has led to a clear and unmistakeable message throughout the Catholic Church.

Cardinal Suenens' openness was seen in the attendance of the media at a luncheon and press conference in his honour. His frankness and sincerity were acknowledged by the journalists who gave him a standing ovation — most unusual in Britain.

At the ceremony in Guildhall the Cardinal broke with tradition and burst into song on two occasions. Hoping to bring the audience of near a thousand with him he diligently persisted but alas a mere handful was able to take part. This, perhaps, was significant for both songs were from the charismatic movement's repertoire and not from *Hymns Ancient and Modern* or other church hymnals.

The presence of Archbishop Basil Hume, recently elevated to the see of Westminster from his Benedictine Abbey, was typical of the openness with which the Cardinal is received in Britain both in his own church and others. Sikh, Hindu and Muslim leaders from Britain were there to greet this controversial churchman as one who had brought enlightenment and hope to a community of people. The unity of Christians in Belgium was in evidence at the

Guildhall ceremony when the President of the Synod of the Belgian Protestant Church, the Reverend Dr André Pieters, was a member of the platform party and pronounced the Benediction.

In her portrait of Cardinal Suenens, Elizabeth Hamilton said: ' "To hope is not to dream, but to turn dreams into reality." The words are those of Leon Joseph Cardinal Suenens, Archbishop of Malines-Brussels. And again he says: "Happy are those who have the courage to dream dreams; who are ready to pay the price, so that their dreams may take shape in the lives of men."

'A dreamer but also a realist, the Primate of Belgium has been, since boyhood, deeply concerned for truth and justice. He is no less concerned for the well-being, spiritual and material, of his fellowmen, regardless of nationality or religious beliefs. Courageous, compassionate, gentle, humorous, he commends the Gospel message in a manner acceptable to our times.

'A major figure throughout the Second Vatican Council and the critical years that followed, he is, today, possibly the greatest spiritual leader of our era. At the close of the Charismatic Congress held in Rome in June 1975, Pope Paul publicly thanked him, not in his own name nor in that of the Church, but in the name of Christ, for all he has done and is doing in the sphere of Charismatic Renewal to make known the reality of the Holy Spirit at work in the world and within each one of us.

'The Cardinal's episcopal motto "In Spiritu Sanctu" is more than a felicitous phrase. These are words for life. They are also a key to an understanding of his way of thought and his actions. It is in the power of the Holy Spirit that he has proclaimed unflaggingly on the continent of Europe, in England, Ireland, the United States, Canada and Latin America, a message of hope, love and joy.

'Of the Holy Spirit he has written:

He is the beginning and the end.
He is the love from whom the world
Came into being.
He is the love who one day will be
All in all.

'The Cardinal's thought bears at every level the stamp of "togetherness", cohesion, unity: Father, Son, and Holy Spirit, the saints, all Christians, the whole world, united in a Triune Deity.

'The God whom the Cardinal commends to us is the God revealed in Jesus: the God who loves each one of us with the totality of his love; knows each one of us by name; keeps us in all our ways.

'In a Christmas prayer the Cardinal asks that we be given a heart capable of loving, a heart of flesh, not stone, so that we may love others not with our frail human love but with the love of Christ. The Holy Spirit can teach us to love. Praying with us, he can teach us to pray. Making his dwelling in our hearts, he can bring visible unity between divided Christians—teaching us to look, together, upon the living face of Christ, to say together: "Jesus is Lord."

'The Cardinal bids us have faith in the Holy Spirit who has promised to lead us into the fulness of truth. He bids us not be afraid: fear denotes lack of faith. He bids us rejoice, that our joy may be full.

'This, in belief, is the message of Léon Joseph Cardinal Suenens, a man of vision, a harbinger of hope, a servant of the Holy Spirit.' (Adapted from *Cardinal Suenens, A Portrait* by Elizabeth Hamilton, Hodder and Stoughton, London; Doubleday, New York.)

The key to the Guildhall ceremony was found in the opening prayer by the Bishop of London, the Right Reverend Gerald A. Ellison, when he led the people to 'be led by the Holy Spirit to have a right judgement in all things as in olden times God did teach the hearts of his faithful people by sending to them the light of the Holy Spirit.'

A secretary listening to the speeches and after reading of his book, said: 'The trouble with this man is that he has done too much.' Cardinal Suenens has indeed achieved in his lifetime results unexcelled by any other reformer in his church and any other group of reformers in his church. Indeed he has not yet finished for he announced at Guild-hall that he will use the money associated with the Prize to support a centre for unity and spiritual renewal in Brussels. He told those present that his hope was that it would contribute to bringing nearer and nearer to each other all those who believe in God. He said the Lord was asking — 'with impatient patience — to hasten the day of visible unity among all Christians.' He saw such a task not being 'the result of a merely human dialogue between men of goodwill,' nor 'the result of some diplomatic compromise,' but rather the unity would be 'found in the heart and in the truth of God Himself,' and will be 'the fruit of our spiritual renewal and of intense and common prayer.'

The Cardinal emphasized that the tragedy of our time is atheism and that the world is 'sick unto death' of it. And that 'a world without God can only end by being a world hostile to men.' He said today 'the depths of inhumanity are marked by the sinister symbols of the concentration camps and show the extent to which the world is thrown off its axis, has lost its centre of cohesion and unity.'

At a private ceremony at Buckingham Palace where His Royal Highness the Duke of Edinburgh presented the award to Cardinal Suenens, Mr Edmund de Rothschild, a judge, in introducing Cardinal Suenens, said that the Cardinal was one of 'those rare creative men with a vision and a capacity for translating that vision into a reality.' Mr de Rothschild said that in recent years the Cardinal's concern for peace with justice for the oppressed peoples and his profound leadership in the charismatic movement has led on un-paralleled lines to renewal in the life and witness of the Church.

Address by the Right Hon. Mrs Margaret Thatcher, M.P.

I am deeply honoured to be your Chairman today, the more particularly because, in this country we rightly put Church before State, and I represent only the State, or at least part of it.

The role of the State is limited. We can make laws about what people must or must not do and we can exact penalties or impose punishments if they do not conform.

But no legislation can make people kind, thoughtful or unselfish to one another or to have courage in the face of fear.

These are the great virtues which come from something far more profound than the actions of governments.

They have a deeply religious foundation — a faith that believes in the essential dignity and importance of each and every human being and that he has a purpose to fulfil here on earth.

Without that religious base, many of the qualities which we take so much for granted, truth, fairness, justice, tolerance, understanding would soon wither and die, like a flower cut off from its root.

But we do not have faith in our own particular religion just because of the social benefits that result.

I remember as a student reading some of C. S. Lewis's books — books which had they been written recently would undoubtedly have found favour one year with your panel of judges. I remember the analogy he used.

That life is like a convoy of many ships. To sail without trouble, the ships had to stay in the right relationship with each other; but to do that each ship has to be in good order itself; and however well the fleet sailed it had to know where it was going.

And so morality seemed to be concerned with three things. Firstly, with fair play and harmony between individuals. Secondly, with harmonizing things outside each individual and thirdly and most important with the purpose of human life and the power that created it.

94

It is this purpose which is the difference between those who have a faith and those who do not.

In the state, we define progress in the cold terms of statistics. In religion progress is far more difficult to elucidate, but perhaps less difficult to recognize.

To you, Mr Templeton, we owe our continuing gratitude for your inspiration and your action in establishing the Templeton Prize for Progress in Religion now to be awarded for the fourth time.

How right you were when you wrote that 'there is a demand today for a deeper awareness of the dimension of the spirit and of the spiritual resources that are available to mankind.'

Recently we have had a similar powerful message on our television sets from Alexander Solzhenitsyn; a message which warned us that failures may be due more to lack of will than to surrounding circumstances; and that true progress would come from a spiritual revival rather than an economic recipe.

His own bravery has been chronicled and we marvel at it. But there must be many thousands of others, unknown heroes and heroines, who refused to yield their beliefs for experience; who show in their daily lives that indomitable spirit which is the hand of Providence.

There is much unhappiness in the world today arising from poverty, disease and ignorance and perhaps even more tragically from conflicts between tribes, ideologies and even religious faiths.

The challenge to statesmen and people alike is daunting.

But in the Christian religion we are taught: 'In the World we shall have tribulation, but be of good cheer.'

And so it was that our first prizewinner, Mother Teresa, went about the business of solving the problems which confronted her. All who have read her moving words or who know of her work have been refreshed and invigorated as they go about their own daily tasks. Such a giant of a person housed in such a tiny body.

Today, we are met to honour a great teacher, Cardinal Suenens, a man whose whole character exemplifies what he has described as 'the living, serene faith'.

His biographer Elizabeth Hamilton writes of his openness, yet of his sense of sensibility to the traditions of the Church.

Sir, all your teachings, and books you have published over the years, stamp you as a theologian of great distinction and scholarship.

But it is for your latest work, *A New Pentecost*, its message and its inspiration, that the distinguished panel of judges has so rightly recommended that the Templeton Foundation present you with its fourth annual award.

Many in the past have applauded and welcomed your advocacy of Christian unity, your encouragement of the Ecumenical movement.

Many, too, have supported your endeavour to re-emphasize the potential and significance of the laity in Church affairs, and many in consequence have been enabled and encouraged to take a greater part in its activities.

Now, as a direct result of the clear and unmistakable message you have given, tens of thousands of individuals in a thousand different Catholic Churches have established groups which are devoted missionaries and witnesses of their faith.

No wonder then that Pope Paul in 1974 saw fit to warmly commend this work and to draw wide attention to it.

Historically, we know that great European civilizations have arisen and then declined.

Each has been dominated by people of great vigour and confidence. And then somehow, those qualities which gave that culture its vitality and inspiration seemed gradually to wither.

But it would be wrong to look at the history of Europe as a history of repeated decline. For each time, a new civilization arose.

Rather it is a testimonial to the strength and inspiration of the human spirit.

No prison or captivity can confine it.

Its vitality will break through the shackles, and the great human endeavour revives and surges forward anew.

You give us, Cardinal Suenens, not only an example but a message and a sense of hope.

'Be of good courage, the power of the Holy Spirit is at work deep within the heart of his Church, breathing into it a great youthfulness.

'It is the spirit who is our living hope for the future.'

Address by Mr John M. Templeton

Your Eminence, Your Grace, Mrs Thatcher, Your Excellencies, My Lords, Ladies and Gentlemen:

It is a joy to be gathered here today in Guildhall for an address by Cardinal Suenens. Nine learned judges from five major religious faiths have awarded to Cardinal Suenens the 1976 Prize for Progress in Religion because of his unique interpretation of New Pentecostal experiences recently occurring in thousands of Roman Catholic churches worldwide.

In addition to those whose names appear on the programme, it is also a joy to have with us today His Grace the Archbishop Athenagoras of Thyateira, representing His All Holiness Demetrios, one of the judges; Mr Henri Perdieus of the Belgian Embassy representing Her Majesty Fabiola, Queen of the Belgians; Mr Edmund de Rothschild, a judge.

We are grateful to His Royal Highness Prince Philip for presenting the fourth annual Prize for Progress in Religion to Cardinal Suenens yesterday at Buckingham Palace, and to Mrs Thatcher for taking the chair at this public ceremony today.

There is a wide variety among those receiving this award in earlier years; but each has done something new and unique which widens or deepens Man's love of God or Man's understanding of God.

Mother Teresa of Calcutta has provided a new understanding of the word 'love'. Brother Roger, founder of the Taizé Community in France, in revitalizing religion among young people of all denominations and confessions. Sir Sarvepalli Radhakrishnan, former President of India, made a unique breakthrough in religion and philosophy and between Eastern and Western religions.

Purpose of Prize

This award programme was created to help people see more clearly the wonderful progress now occurring in all major religions. God seems to be revealing himself more and more rapidly.

Astronomers say our galaxy called the Milky Way contains thousands of millions of stars and planets. Each is a little piece of God. Until recently, no one dreamed that each star is larger than the earth. Astronomers believe that the Universe contains more than five million other galaxies. Not only is God creating the vast universe but if God is infinite, then the Universe is not separate from God, but rather an outward manifestation of God Himself. If God is infinite, then nothing exists separate from God. Mankind has learned more about the Universe in this century than in the other 180 million centuries since God began His creation of the Universe.

Astronomers are beginning to develop a theology based on this knowledge. They are giving us a new understanding of the meaning of the words 'infinite' and 'eternal'. Some day, possibly, the judges may award this annual Prize for Progress in Religion to an astronomer.

More than half the natural scientists who ever lived are living today. Their increasing discoveries are in reality discoveries about God. Recent discoveries in nuclear physics cause some scientists to say that the earth is more accurately described not as a solid mass of particles, but rather a 'wave pattern' or 'symphony of life' or an 'unfolding idea'. Things which are not seen may be more numerous and more awe-inspiring than things which are seen. When scientists stand in awe of the Creative Spirit of the Universe, they are very close to worship. Already, respected scientists are beginning to study the nature of religious experience. Some day, the judges may award this Prize to a scientist who discovers new concepts or new instruments which multiply Man's ability to see the unseen, because each new discovery is only a little part of the infinite God.

Infinite God

If God is infinite, then God is all of us and we are tiny part of Him. Geneticists are now making multitudes of discoveries about how God's creatures reproduce themselves. God is revealing Himself to geneticists, as well as to the astronomers. Probably soon, geneticists may build insects and humans with wierd and wonderful shapes and abilities. The geneticists are created by God; and maybe this is a new step in God's creation of His Universe whereby the slow process of evolution is speeded up. Some geneticists wonder if they are worthy tools in God's hands, when they are given this new and awesome power to change life's basic processes. Already some deep thinking is beginning about the philosophy and the theology of geneticists. Perhaps some day the judges may select a geneticist to receive this Award, as one of the persons who has done most to increase Man's understanding of God.

Each of us should be deeply grateful that God allowed us to be born in this generation when the quantity of knowledge is increasing and accelerating. Much evidence has been found that God's ongoing creative process is accelerating. Even this acceleration seems to be accelerating. The accelerating discovery rate in natural sciences needs to be matched by Man's spiritual progress and discovery. This could happen if religious organizations budgeted enough resources and brains towards spiritual research. If we humbly admit how little we know, perhaps we will become more diligent in searching and learning.

Maybe only part of your soul dwells in your body. Maybe your body is created as a schoolroom for your soul. Some Christians say that the reason you are on this earth is to become more Christlike and to help others become more Christlike. Maybe your marvellous brain is the connecting link between body and soul; but your brain is equipped to sense or store only a tiny fraction of the waves which pass through your body. Maybe when God said He made Man in God's image, He meant that Man is not only created by God, but shares in some small way in the creative process. Each of us should be grateful that God is allowing us to help as little creators in His tremendous and expanding creation. Some say that He even allows us to participate in the training of our souls and to create our own individual heaven or hell here and now.

Greater humility is needed about our knowledge of God. He is infinite and we are very tiny and limited. No man may ever know even one per cent of the infinite creative Spirit. To learn more, first we must become humble and rid ourselves of the egotistical idea that we know it all about God already.

Humility teaches us not to despise any other child of God because he worships God in a different way. Differences are helpful because thereby each of us can learn a little more about God. Not only should we love each other, but also listen to each other. Surely, we can learn from one another. We need not fear to exchange ideas, because if your idea is truth, it will endure. The myriad forms of life on earth now show us that both variety and progress are part of God's plan.

Let me conclude with the words of Cardinal Suenens when he was asked why he is a man of hope. Cardinal Suenens said :

Because I believe that God is born anew each morning; because I believe that He is creating the world at this very moment. He did not create it long ago in the past, then forget about it. It is happening now. We must therefore be ready to expect the unexpected from God. The ways of Providence are by nature surprising. We are not prisoners of determinism nor of the sombre prognostications of sociologists. God is here, near us, unforeseeable and loving. I am a man of hope, not for human reasons nor from natural optimism, but because I believe the Holy Spirit is at work in the Church and in the world, even where His name remains unheard.

Address by His Eminence Leon Joseph Cardinal Suenens

My first word of gratitude must go to the Lord for having inspired Mr Templeton to create this Foundation. And my second word of thanks must go to Mr Templeton for having accepted this inspiration of which I myself am the beneficiary today.

'The objective of the Templeton Prize — as we know it — is to stimulate the knowledge and love of God on the part of mankind everywhere. Such an attitude and such a relationship have their own intrinsic value.'

In stressing that we are created to know, to love and to serve God — and to make him known and loved and served, Mr Templeton has given his Foundation a message for mankind.

In a world where the idea of civilization is so often reduced to mere progress in comfort, in wealth, in power, it is important that the role and the place of religion should be stressed, to re-establish the right scale of values.

All of us are grateful for Mr Templeton's initiative, for his vision, for his spiritual courage.

The Templeton Prize is awarded on the decision of a panel of nine judges, who are representative of the major faiths of the world today.

My thanksgiving goes especially to those distinguished judges for their kindness to me. I see in their decision, for myself, an invitation from the Lord to open more and more my personal religious concern to the full dimension of humanity and the world's religions.

The Conditions of Society Today

Wherever men believe in a supreme, immanent and transcendent Being, in a Supreme Lover of men, we find the deepest ground of human fellowship, we discover the final basis for peace and brotherhood among men.

And who will deny that peace is the most urgent need of mankind? When we look at the world of today, we cannot avoid that a feeling of anguish, even sometimes of despair, comes over us. Where are we going? What will happen with mankind if tomorrow somebody just pushes a button to bring about the apocalyptic nuclear explosion? What will happen tomorrow to a human being, if society can and will manipulate a person from conception till the end of human life and if the collectivity can decide in supreme liberty, without reference to any higher moral principles, what is right or wrong? Where are we going when moral pollution is increasing everyday? More than ever we feel the need to recognize all together that there is a power, stronger than nuclear energy, the loving presence of a Supreme Spirit, who guides mankind.

The stability of a building depends on its foundation and its cornerstone. And God is still today the origin and the end of man and society. The man who denies God repeats the actions of Samson and brings down the edifice around him. It is not possible to build up humanity first and then give it to God, as one might first erect a building, and afterwards decide on the use to which it shall be put. If the stones of society are to hold together, they must be buttressed on God. It is an illusion to believe that human society can stand independent of the Creator.

Hans Anderson tells the story of a spider which, after

spinning a beautiful web, thought to free itself from the thread which fastened it to the branch, and snapped the seemingly unnecessary link. The result was that the web fell to pieces, because its centre and heart had been torn out. It is the same for human society centred on God. Adhesion to God brings about social cohesion; the vertical line is essential to the stability of the cross threads.

The world is sick unto death of its atheism. That is the tragedy of our time. It is not true, as is sometimes said, that men cannot organize a world without God. But what is true is that a world without God can only end by being a world hostile to men. We have reached that stage today. Since men have ceased to know God, they have more and more to be defended against one another — *homo homini lupus* (man is a wolf to man). The depths of inhumanity marked by the sinister symbol of the concentration camps show the extent to which the world is thrown off its axis, has lost its centre of cohesion and unity. When man has obstinately rejected God, the direst fate that can overtake man is to be delivered over to man.

Some years ago, Carl Jung wrote a famous statement that has been repeated often since, showing by his own experience as a psychologist how God is the vital source of our being, our 'innermost self'. In his book *Modern Man in Search of a Soul*, he said these striking words: 'During the past thirty years, people from all the civilized countries of earth have consulted me. . . . Among my patients in the second half of life — that is to say over thirty-five years — there has not been one whose problem in the last resort was not that of finding a religious outlook on life. It is safe to say that everyone of them fell ill because he had lost that which the living religions of every age have given to their followers. Not one of them has been really healed who had not regained this religious outlook.'

The Ecumenical Purpose of the Prize

It is not only my duty to express my deep gratitude to all

of you who take an active part in this ceremony, but I wish also to explain to you what I intend to do with the money so graciously given to me. I will use it to support a centre for unity and spiritual renewal in my own city of Brussels.

Spent in this way, I hope it will contribute to bringing nearer and nearer to each other all those who believe in God, and especially all those who believe in Our Lord and Saviour Jesus Christ. We know how difficult it is to build bridges, but the Lord is asking us—with impatient patience — to hasten the day of visible unity among all Christians. We know too that such a task will not be the result of a merely human dialogue between men of goodwill nor that this unity could be the result of some diplomatic compromise. The ground of our unity lies deeper, our unity is to be found in the heart and in the truth of God Himself; our unity will be the fruit of our spiritual renewal and of intense and common prayer. It has been said: 'More things are wrought by prayer than this world dreams of.' I think this is profoundly true. In my opinion prayer and adoration are essential and decisive elements on our way towards visible unity between all Christians.

Being one, visibly, in prayer, we will be one in a new and powerful way in a common apostolic, social and political action, for the service of the world. We need unity between those who are impatient with prayer, contemplation or worship and who think them to be outmoded and who look to the service of God solely in social and political activism and those who turn rather to mysticism, prayer, contemplation, hungry for union with a reality beyond our narrow immediate limits. We need to bring together those two trends of mind, the political as well as the mystical.

They all belong together. 'The witness of social and political activism, and the witness of prayer and contemplation desperately need each other.'

These words have been said by Bishop Ramsey and we gladly subscribe to them.

United, we will have to face together the world and to offer it what it needs the most: an answer to the social problems of the man of today and an answer to the problems of the man of all times and of all countries, the eternal man hungry for God.

To express it in terms of my own faith, let me say that we have:

to give, at the same time, man-made bread and the Bread of life;

to teach the sciences of men and the science of God;

to offer social security and deep belief in the Providence of God;

to stress the value of work and the value of prayer, the need for social pioneers and for saints, the duty to enter with expectant faith in the silence of the Upper Room and to come out of the Upper Room with the power of the Spirit, into the market place, to proclaim the good news of the Gospel, to hasten the day of glory and joy, announced by the Lord when 'from East and West people will come, from North and South, for the feast is in the Kingdom of God' (Luke 13:29).

SELECTED BIBLIOGRAPHY

Nun in the World, Cardinal Suenens. Burns & Oates, London.

A New Pentecost, Cardinal Suenens. Darton, Longman & Todd, London.

Cardinal Suenens—A Portrait. Elizabeth Hamilton. Hodder & Stoughton, London.

chapter nine

CHIARA LUBICH 1977

The 50's was a decade when one was the bearer of recog-
nised skills. At almost all levels of society the Pastor was
accepted as a professional person with a valid skill.

This concept has now changed. The Second Vatican Council
came and in the person of Pope John 'all windows of
thought and tradition' were open to the breezes of the
twentieth century. John Robinson, then the Bishop of
Woolwich in England, wrote a thought-provoking book
from his hospital bed — called *Honest to God*. And that
caused quite a stir. Other names made the headlines and
all of a sudden the quiet traditional forms of the Christian
Church were in turmoil — for the better.

At this time, unknown to most of Christendom and certainly unknown to the other major religions, there was a
growing group in Italy called the Focolare Movement.
Founded in the northern Italian city of Trent in 1943 this
Movement was to force a highly institutional form of
Christianity to seek ways in which it could find community
even in the face of all that militates against community in
to-day's world.

From European cities to bush villages in the Camaroon and the squalid slums of Recife in north-east Brazil the Movement spread, bringing hope and life to many.

This Movement has brought many to realise that belonging to a Church as an institutional system is not sufficient in to-day's world.

Its founder and leader, Chiara Lubich, with her enchanting charisma, aided the Focolare Movement to become a symbol that membership of the Church through Faith led to an experience of God in one's life that membership in a Church as a system could never achieve.

It is this crucial difference that has aided the Focolare Movement to show an added dimension to the role of the Christian in to-day's world. This is seen in the phrase 'the people of God'. The professionals of the 50's talked of the Church as 'the Body of Christ' but this was, for many, an abstract term and almost impossible to understand. The personal experience of Christ changing lives has the outward and visible sign that is at once meaningful to many people. If anything is the hallmark of the Focolare Movement it is just that.

Another dimension added by the Focolare Movement is the modern concept of the age-old idea of spirituality. It is perhaps this aspect that has attracted other religions to the Focolare Movement. While the traditional form of impersonal spirituality found in different sections of the Christian Church turned young people off Christianity, this new, deeply personal form as exercised by the Focolare Movement has attracted many, and significantly a number of clergy.

The healing hand of God on the lives of individuals and the search for a new Community founded on the basic commandment of Christ 'love one another as I have loved you' have drawn quite a cross-section of modern society to the Focolare Movement — architects, doctors, engineers, nurses, carpenters, secretaries, have all found a sense of belonging together that in the 'run-of-the-mill' society is just not there.

All this did not go unnoticed when Chiara Lubich addressed a crowded Guildhall in London on April 6th. She received a rapturous applause and the media afterwards described her in various ways as a person with hope to offer a stricken world.

And the hope of the Templeton Foundation in awarding the Prize for 1977 to Chiara Lubich is that this ray of hope will ensure that many more will find the experience of God in their lives as one that changes Man and society for the better.

CHIARA LUBICH

We are not living in the age of a great saint
We are living in the age of Jesus;
Jesus present among us,
Jesus living in us.
Who enables us to create the christian community
In a spirit of unity and love.

(C. Lubich)

Like every authentic charism, the charism of Chiara Lubich is at the service of all the human community and it expresses itself through the life and witness of a spiritual family. She has received a special gift from God to create a movement which has unity as its characteristic. The union of a few in order to bring about the unity of many, the unity of two for the unity of all : this is the one aim of every expression of the movement.

Chiara Lubich's spirituality is like a coin which has two faces : on one side there is the search for unity, which is translated into a presence, the presence of Jesus himself which he promised to those who are united in his name (Mt 18, 20); on the other side of the coin, there is the same

108

love, the same Christ but portrayed as the 'crucified God'. The presence of God and the suffering of God; love and suffering are the radically opposed extremes which make up the human experience.

Between the two sides of the coin is all the gospel, all the words of God put into practice every day, discovered afresh in their uniqueness and relevance. This is another fruit of the charism: the re-discovery of the gospel as the word which can illuminate and transform every life and every moment of everyone's life.

'What struck me at the beginning was the freshness of the gospel which the movement gives to the world, this demonstration that the gospel is of burning relevance to-day.' (Cardinal Suenens).

The new commandment is the centre of spirituality of the Focolare Movement, and this relationship of love extends to all men.

'This is the age of the Mystical Body' (Pope Pius XII). It follows therefore that if this age is lived, the repercussions on the life of society will soon be visible. One of the results should be the growth of mutual esteem among states, among peoples. This is not what usually happens. We are used, in fact, to seeing strongly-marked frontiers between peoples; we are used to fearing the power of others. The most we do is form alliances, but only when it is to our own advantage to do so. But popular morality has never reached the level of deciding to act out of love for another people. When, however, the life of the Mystical Body will be so developed among individuals who effectively love their neighbours as themselves, whatever their race, then it will be easy to transplant this law between states.

'A new phenomenon will appear, because love either finds people who love or makes people love. The peoples of the world will learn what is best in each people and the virtues of each people will be circulated so that they all will be enriched. Then truly there will be unity and diversity and a people will flourish which will be a child of the earth, but which can call itself "the people of God", because it is formed by the laws of heaven.' (C. Lubich).

Chiara Lubich has placed herself and her activity at the service of the Church and of ecumenism in order to promote greater unity within the Roman Catholic Church around the Pope, and in ecumenical action in order to promote unity among Christians and amng all men. In an address to members of the movement on March 10th 1971, Pope Paul VI said: 'They are faithful to the Church and God blesses them. It makes us happy to see the fervour they bring everywhere. Theirs is not just a positive adhesion which they try to communicate to others. This is a most consoling phenomenon . . . and one which the Church has great need of to-day.'

Brother Roger Schutz, the Prior of Taize, gave this account of his meeting with Chiara Lubich: 'My meeting with Chiara Lubich left a mark on my soul. Since then I have often seen Chiara again and the transparentness of this woman is like an open page of the gospel. I do not forget that Chiara was chosen from among the humble, the workers, in order to confound the strong, the powerful of this world. And I praise Christ, our Lord for this. I know that by means of women like Chiara, God gives an incomparable instrument of unity to us Christians, separated by a long, centuries old, divorce.'

This is how those who best know her and her work see her. It is also how the world is seeing her. For me she is someone you wish would come on the scene of time amidst the poverty of our affluence and help us to see God as He really is. That is the impression Chiara left with me after a visit to her home on the outskirts of Rome when I went to see her and let her know the decision of the Judges. And I hope it will be that impression that will linger with modern man.

Address by Mrs John M. Templeton

Your Eminence, Your Serene Highness,
Ladies and Gentlemen,

Five years ago, with deep and concentrated humble prayers
this programme was announced to the world. It has been
my great privilege to share in its birth and in its yearly
growth.

It was first an 'idea' in my husband's mind — inspired
partly by the statement of a scientist that said 'when the
history of the twentieth century is written, the new discoveries will be found not in the natural sciences but in
the realm of the Spirit.'

This idea or inspiration grew stronger as it was lovingly
and prayerfully encouraged — Action was the next step,
it had to be the right action, — God's action, and humanly
this is a fine line to walk. As the idea took form and grew,
like a child it needed protective *selfless* prayer, 'The
Father's will, done on earth as it is in heaven.'

This programme was conceived to awaken man, or to
make known to man, new revelations, new ideas about
God — inspiration or thoughts that would enlighten un-
touchable areas.

The miracle or phenomenon of the human mind separates
individuals unlike any other, each dwelling in their own
mental realm, suggests trillions of inspirations or revelations, messages of the Infinite One God and of His
unfathomed LOVE which is constantly feeding mankind
spiritually. Inspirations, thoughts, ideas from the Infinite
One come to us when we are humble, *selfless* and receptive.
This is an experience available to every man, woman and
child. We need only to open our hearts and minds to
God. I know that many here today can testify to this — as
can our award winner.

David, the Psalmist said 'This is the day the Lord hath
made, we will rejoice and be glad in it.' We can truly
rejoice this day as we honour Miss Lubich, a dedicated

twentieth-century disciple of Christ, a follower of the way. In the New Testament in Luke we read that Christ said — 'Whosoever cometh to me and heareth my sayings and doeth them, I will show you to whom he is like.' Chiara Lubich heard His message, 'Love one another as I have loved you.' She was obedient to this instruction and has been influential in bringing joy, peace and love to God's children. She found the Master, heard Him and doeth it.

If each and every Child of God lives his or her under-standing to its highest degree it is seen in their daily human experience and is visible proof to the unbeliever. As in the lives of Mother Teresa, Brother Roger, Sarvepalli Radha-krishnan, Cardinal Suenens and the winner this year of the Templeton Programme of Prizes for Progress in Religion, Chiara Lubich—who can doubt the consummate example?

Address by John Cardinal Willebrands
President of Secretarial for Christian Unity

When I accepted, with a proper sense of the honour done to me, your invitation to preside at the giving of the Templeton prize to Chiara Lubich, I naturally thought of the distinguished people who had both presented and re-ceived the prize in earlier years. I was immediately struck by a remark made by His Royal Highness the Duke of Edinburgh when he presented the prize to that other great Catholic woman of our time, Mother Teresa. In his usual stimulating and forthright way His Royal Highness ob-served that 'At first sight the idea that a prize might be able to do something for religion seems faintly absurd.' The remark is thought-provoking. It might not perhaps arouse many scruples among those hard-pressed pastors who anxiously watch your English weather on the days of their garden-parties, but even apart from our Lord's exhortation that we should lay up treasures in heaven

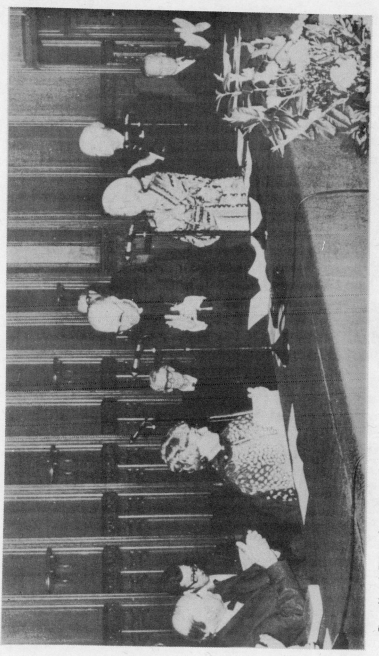

Cardinal Willebrands (centre) and platform party applaud Chiara Lubich the winner of the 1977 award.

His Royal Highness, Prince Philip presents the award to Chiara Lubich. In the centre is Dr Dimitri Bregant, leader of the Focolare Movement in England.

rather than on earth, the notion of giving a prize of this kind might suggest a claim to interior spiritual knowledge that only the Lord Himself could make.

But these are reserves which, as His Royal Highness said, we entertain only at first sight. There is a deeper view of the matter. Many public prizes are nowadays offered in many fields, for achievements which are publicly manifest and of benefit to humanity. These are a healthy counter-balance to the extravagant financial rewards which contemporary fashion dictates should go to very frivolous accomplishments, and which not even the tax-man can keep within reasonable boundaries. A public prize — like the Templeton — is more than a gain to the recipient — it is a public confession of a scale of values, a public witness that, as St. Paul says, 'none of us lives to himself, and none of us dies to himself' (Rom. xiv, 7), and that all men fulfil themselves most surely in putting others before themselves — an order of priorities for which Christianity offers the profoundest basis. It is on the particular way in which the choice of Chiara Lubich for this year's award reflects this scale of values and this witness that I want to dwell for a short time.

The Fireside Movement

My starting point must be the very name of the movement which she founded — the Focolare, the Fireside movement. Here we might see another apparent paradox: the fireside is not the first place we associate with movement. It is that immemorial point of light and warmth round which the family gathers in unity, understanding and love. It is an admirable symbol of the deep biological and spiritual instinct that makes men see all human unity, so that we use words like 'family of nations', 'world confessional family' and finally the 'human family' to express ideals which broaden out from the fireside, from the home. Indeed the very notion of the human family would be an unmanageable abstraction, a rhetorical tool for globetrotting publicists, if it were not rooted in the experience of people living together, sharing in love.

I need not tell you what part this idea of the family has played in Christianity. The central truths of our faith, the Trinity and the Incarnation are bound up with it. God, the Father of us all, sent His divine Son to take on our nature, and thirty years of his life were spent in the family of Nazareth, the hidden life centred on a *focolare* preparing for the mere three years which fill the New Testament. Yet nothing does more than a contemplation of the Gospel story to dissolve the apparent paradox of a *fireside movement*. The family as an institution is permanent, instructive, but each family in a sense comes into being only that it may disperse. The family creates bonds which are seldom wholly broken, but it is also a school of living and growing, and one does not stay in school for ever. The strength of the family is a strength on which we draw to face many challenges — perhaps to found another literal family — a task which today brings enough of its own problems — perhaps to find new sources of strength in other associations far from our 'hearth'. As one of your modern poets has put it, 'Home is where one starts from.'

Apostolic Brotherhood

The apostolic brotherhood itself, gathered always round the master, had much of the character of a family, expressed most of all in the Lord's supper, the model for the central act of the liturgy. Liturgical reform has thrown once more into relief how the communion of the local Church, gathered around its president for the celebration of the Lord's Supper, presents in itself the fullness of the universal Church. It was from this heart of strength that the apostles and disciples had dispersed to preach the Gospel and to establish new communities of love.

It is not surprising then that in Christian history (though not only there) the concept of family has powerfully influenced those wider associations which have at many points in history sprung up to meet the crisis of an age. The most distinguished of Methodist historians, Gordon Rupp, speaking of St. Benedict, has reminded us that

> at the heart of the Christian religion is the beloved community, the *koinonia*, the Christian group or cell; and the secret of true community is not in the casual brushing shoulders of the streets of the secular city, or of dwellers in flats or seaside hotels. The Benedictine rule is for a common life, because Christianity is a team game, because its virtues cannot be exercised in a vacuum or grown in isolation, but need a Christian family small enough for its members to know one another very well indeed, to watch over one another, to bear with one another's weaknesses and rejoice in one another's victories.
>
> G. Rupp, *Just Men*, p. 5

It is surely no accident that one of Francis of Assisi's humanising strokes of genius was to popularise the image of Bethlehem, the Christmas crib. His intuition of the brotherhood of men, and of nature too, in Christ was of endless fertility and has appealed to men of every age and sort, but it was even more strongly rooted in simplicity, in the belief that 'small is beautiful', so that he feared the very consequences of its success — enlargement, stability, institutionalisation.

These are only two eminent examples of the tradition of Christian renewal, of response to new needs. In both of them, as in many others, we see how an outward and forward thrust, a renewal of evangelical energy has drawn strength from being embodied in a family, and hence embodying what is a fundamental human as well as Christian value. The power of God, of the Spirit, has no bounds, geographical or other, but when it works through men and women it is bound to the realities of human living, which are as intimate and particular as love. We see that to say 'Home is where one starts from' is theologically profound. The same poet has told us that when we live in what he calls 'a place of disaffection' (whatever it is that has destroyed our communion) then there is

'. . . Only a flicker
over the strained, time-ridden faces
Distracted from distraction by distraction . . .
Men and bits of paper, whirled by the cold wind.'

If we look at the Focolare movement with these thoughts in mind, what do we see?

One of Chiara Lubich's most moving utterances was made near Rome less than a year ago, when she spoke to an ecumenical assembly on the theme 'Jesus in Our Midst', with clear reference to the text of Matthew XVIII, 20: 'Where two or three are gathered together in my name there am I in their midst.' Now she has told us elsewhere how she and her early companions saw their common aim as that of 'taking the Gospel seriously' — a revolutionary programme they called it, and which of us will question the description? Chiara tells us, speaking of the text of Matthew, 'when the movement first came to life in 1943, in Catholic environments there wasn't much talk about the presence of Jesus in our midst.' In the lecture I speak of, she sets out to see what the text meant to the Fathers of the Church, what their meditation on it can contribute to its fruitfulness for our time. But impressive though this study is, it is nothing beside what she and her helpers have created in our society in so many places, in living response to Christ's assurance and Christ's appeal. The focolare movement is an example, visible to all, stirring many, comforting many more, of a world-wide growth which is realistic because it is from small beginnings, rooted in reality, the reality of two or three gathered seriously in Christ's name. The response to the call to take the Gospel seriously is not to be made with mere words — this truth

116

is part of the Gospel itself. For too many of us the words of the Gospel that are most often appropriate on our lips are those put into the mouth of the timid disciples: 'This is a hard saying — who shall listen to it?' (John VI, 60). But common, unifying resolve, issuing in a way of life, may make the 'revolutionary programme' a reality, small at first, but with vast potentiality for growth. A commentator on the *focolare* has written that 'in all the expressions of the movement one aim can be found: the union of a few to bring about the unity of many.' Most revolutions sooner or later divide and destroy, but the revolution of a return to the Gospel unites and builds up, so that we find the New Testament itself constantly speaking of the building up of the Church and of oneness in Christ. An invitation to take the Gospel seriously is an invitation first to go home, to go to our family roots in Christ, but to draw strength to set out again on the true way. Indeed, this revolution of taking the Gospel seriously is often expressed in an even more radical image in the New Testament: for the Christian the drama of death is not primarily that of bodily death, that launching into the shades, into the unknown which so frightened the ancients and which we all bend so much ingenuity to postpone. For the Christian, the true dying, the true entering into new life is baptism into Christ.

Prize for Progress

The Templeton prize is given for '*progress* in religion'. Can we judge, can we observe 'progress in religion'? If there is any meaning on earth to Christ's words, 'By their fruits you shall know them', the answer must be yes. To invite men and women to take the Gospel seriously, to die in order to rise to its life, and then to provide a family setting in which they may do so with joy — this is progress, this is the increase which God gives. Christian history has not been exempt from stagnation, from hardening of the arteries, from the petrification of institutions which began under the impulse of love and of zeal, but the eternal source of the Gospel is manifest in the continual capacity for renewal, for generating new life. The New Testament is full of the language of renewal, rebirth. The Christian religion is not a static one: if there is no progress to note and praise — in thought, in spiritual life, in worship, in art, above all in the communal realisation of the Gospel, the outlook is grim. It was the realisation of this that made men far beyond the bounds of the Church of Rome welcome and thank God for the Second Vatican Council. Christian progress is always a return to the sources; this is not historical revivalism or antiquarianism, because the sources are eternal, and so eternally relevant, eternally capable of revitalising society in any situation. In the course of history, it has often seemed necessary, and always attractive, to create a new community, a new family on the model of the Gospel. This has always required courage. To do it in the forest and hills after the fall of the Roman Empire, or in the first century after the discovery of America, called for backbreaking work and willingness to face danger, discouragement, destruction. But who shall say that it requires less courage and not more, to create a family, or a family of families, in the light of a great vision like the Gospel here in the heart of the technological society, in the midst of a civilisation which to many seems itself to be suffering from loss of nerve. Chiara Lubich herself has said, significantly, that the focolarini of Fontem in the Cameroun 'seem to understand the real meaning of our movement better than the Christians of Europe and America.'

But whenever Christian courage is found, it is not a self-regarding and solemn posture. It is modelled on Christ, and so its driving-force is love, self-giving, and its sign is serenity. The mere list of *Focolare* foundations in a span of thirty years speaks of courage and tenacity, but the Christian stamp of that courage, which is serenity and love, can only be seen in the *life* of those foundations. I need not apologise for the example I choose to illustrate this: The Focolare movement realised its ecumenical potential through an encounter with Lutherans in 1960, the same year in which the Roman Secretariat for Promoting Christian Unity was founded. The Anglican meeting with and participation in the movement was even more strikingly a result of a chance encounter in Rome. When the Anglo/Roman Catholic International Commission, tackling a difficult phase of its work, looked for a meeting-place in 1974, it was not surprising that it should turn to the beautiful Mariapolis near Grottaferrata. Many members of the commission have said that this meeting had a unique atmosphere, the happiest they had experienced, and that it seemed something communicated to them by the focolarini, not only in their devoted hospitality and help, their interest and prayers, but simply in the spectacle of Christian serenity which they presented at every moment. A small example, but an important one. Much earlier Michael Ramsey, after a talk with Chiara Lubich at Lambeth, had put his finger with his usual precision on the same point. He said:

> There are many ways and means by which you can work together with Anglicans and have spiritual communion with them in this country, so that their *hearts may be warmed* by the fire of this spirit.

Heart-warming

Heart-warming: a good word for focolarini, and a description of a need that is always indispensable to ecumenism. Unless our common baptism, our common commitment to Christ warms our hearts so that the warmth communicates itself across the barriers we have grown up with, theological dialogue will never draw us to that 'focus' which will make us fully one family in Christ.

'So,' as St. Pauls says, 'if there is any encouragement in Christ, any incentive of love, any participation in the

Spirit, any affection and sympathy, complete my joy by being of the same mind, having the same love, being in full accord and of one mind.' (Phil. II, 1-2).

✝ JOHN CARDINAL WILLEBRANDS

Address by Chiara Lubich

Your Eminence, Ladies and Gentlemen,
I think you would like me to present to you my experience of faith and of life which goes hand in hand with the birth and development of the Focolare Movement on account of which I am here today. But all this requires a premise.

In 1968 I was right in the middle of the forest in a remote region of the Cameroon among the Bangwa tribe, which was dying out because of the high infant mortality rate. Three of my friends had gone there before me in order to bring some help to the tribe who had nothing. I had the opportunity of talking to the Fon, the chief of the tribe, a wise man, who, although knowing very little about the world, had been informed however about the Focolare Movement.

He was impressed by the fact that it had spread to all five continents, and he asked me a question in the following terms: 'You are a woman and therefore are worth nothing. Tell me, how did all this happen? You are a woman, and therefore are worth nothing.' Faced with this phrase, I assure you I felt perfectly at ease, knowing that all I was going to tell him was certainly not the work of a woman, but the work of God.

The Focolare Movement — as Pope Paul VI said some years ago — is a tree which is now rich and very fruitful. A tree. Certainly. And as we all know, even the most majestic trees are born from a seed.

Trent, 1943

Let's go back thirty-four years to 1943, to the quiet little city of Trent in Northern Italy. I was a teacher and I was giving private lessons to help my family which was passing through a period of extreme poverty. I was twenty-three years old. One day, while helping someone out of love, I felt an unexpected call: 'Give yourself to God.' A few days later, I offered my life for ever to the Lord. My happiness was boundless. No one knew about it. No plan for my life came into my head. I belonged to God: this was enough for me. Outwardly it was a day like any other. But my soul was invaded by a particular grace, a flame had been lit. And if the flame is lit, it cannot but burn, it must communicate itself. A few days later some other girls followed me.

The 13th May 1944. Trent was not spared by the war which raged in the whole of Italy. That night when the air raid siren sounded I fled with my family to a nearby wood and we could hear the noise of the planes and the bombs bursting. From a piece of high ground I could see the houses around mine collapsing. I understood that it was the moment to leave Trent. But I could not leave. Who would have kept in contact with my young friends, who were bound to me by such a strong bond? How could I abandon them and stay in the city. I remembered a phrase. It applied in my case too: 'Love conquers all.' *All*. Yes, I will be able to leave my family, even in these terrible circumstances, in order to follow a way which I as yet do not know. At dawn, with courage, we returned to our ruined house. I told my father my secret; I belong to God and there are others who follow me. I cannot abandon them. He understood me and blessed me. While my family moved off towards the mountains I moved off towards the centre of the stricken city. Ruins. Silence. I searched. All my friends were alive. They ranged in age from fifteen to twenty-five.

The war continued. Many things were destroyed. Many ideals collapsed which had occupied our young minds. One of us loved her home — and it was destroyed. Another loved her fiancé — and the boy never returned from the front. I was studying at a university in another city — I could not continue. Whoever had taken art as their ideal saw valuable works shattered in an instant. We used to meet together every day, even eleven times a day, in the air-raid shelter which, however, was not safe. We could have died from one moment to the next. A question pressed strongly on us. But surely there must be an ideal which does not die, which is worth being followed and which no bomb can destroy. The answer came immediately : Yes — God. Let's make God the ideal of our life then. But time is limited : how many days or hours will we still have for living according to this new ideal? I took the Gospel with me into the air raid shelter. I opened it. Those words which we had often heard seemed to light up one by one and gave us a very new understanding of things. They were truly words of life suited to everyone. One day we felt a strong desire : is there a word of Christ which particularly pleased Him? If we were to present ourselves shortly before Jesus, we would like to have lived what He had most at heart. We recalled His last farewell, when He gave His apostles a command which He calls 'my' and 'new' : 'This is my commandment : that you love one another as I have loved you. No one has greater love than this : to give his life for his own friends.' (John 15 : 12-13). We felt these holy words in us like fire. We looked at one another and declared to each other : 'I am ready to die for you, I for you, I for you : All for each of us.' Since we were ready therefore to die, it was not difficult there and then to each day share our sufferings and our joys, our new spiritual experiences, and our poor possessions. Mutual love was placed as the foundation for everything. And, because of this, among those few girls, God was present, He who said 'Where two or three are gathered together in

my name, I am there among them.' (Matthew 18 : 20).
But when God is present and you allow God to act, things
do not remain as they were before. The terrible situations
which surrounded us were like a training field which
brought love into action not only among us, but among all
those who passed next to us. The Gospel continued to
direct our behaviour and we realised that with it, a revolution was born. 'Love your neighbour *as* yourself' (Matthew 19 : 19). As yourself — this is something new. 'Love
your enemies' (Matthew 5 : 44). Who had considered this?
'May they all be one' (John 17 : 21). All.

New Awareness

People became aware of this new style of life : above all
of a joy which shone from the faces of those girls and
which was not in contrast with a full participation in the
general suffering. People asked for an explanation, were
convinced, and united with us. After a few months there
were 500 of us living for the same ideal : God. In our hearts
the terror of the war faded. The light of God shone out
more strongly.
One day a phrase in the Gospel struck us : 'Anyone who
listens to you listens to me' (Luke 10 : 16). Jesus addressed
this phrase to the Apostles. Yes, everything was born so
spontaneously. But the bishop, the apostle today, he who
represents God, does he know about it? Will he be happy?
We presented ourselves to him, ready to destroy all that
had been done directly he requested it. The bishop concluded : 'Here there is the finger of God.'
The war ended. We could travel again. But who could take
away from our heart what God had marked on it? The
circumstances of life, study, work, the family, took one or
other of us to different cities in Italy. Wherever one of
us arrived, a phenomenon similar to the one in Trento
occurred. Groups were born silently, of people who wanted
to live the Gospel.

The promises it offers are fascinating and extraordinary but it does not deceive. It is possible to follow Jesus — what greater adventure can there be — on condition that we renounce ourselves and take up our own cross (cf. Luke 9 : 23). This is an experience we make every day. We will have eternal life and the hundredfold already in this life, in terms of brothers, sisters, fathers, mothers, houses, and work, but in the midst of persecutions, but we must be detached at least spiritually from everything (cf. Mark 10 : 29-30). The Movement is a living witness that the promises of Jesus actually come true. It has lived and will always live the Gospel in its aspects of suffering and marvellous joy.

The Focolare Movement went ahead irresistibly. At its heart there are little communities of a new style called focolari, made up of men or women, who are joined so far as is possible, by married people who strongly desire holiness. (At present there are 217 focolari in 33 countries, and a total of 2,400 focolarini). God, step by step, inspired an ordering of the movement. This was logical. Those involved with it by now are not just young women and men, but people from every sort of social background, and also priests, religious, and nuns. Among the most committed lay people, after the focolarini, come the volunteers. They live in their own homes, and live the same spirit, with set commitments.

Became International

The movement crossed frontiers : first it spread to all the countries of Europe, then from 1958 onwards it spread in an extraordinary way to more than 100 countries and hundreds of thousands of people.

The Church in Rome, with its centuries old wisdom, studied the new movement. In 1962 Pope John XXIII gave the first approval, and Pope Paul VI gave further approvals because there were new developments in the movement. A period began of profound joy and of gratitude to God who guides all things. Before the approvals were granted it may be said that both the movement as a whole and each individual member of it had lived the phrase: 'Unless the grain of wheat which has fallen to the ground dies, it remains alone' (John 12 : 24). But the members of the movement tried to be ready to die to themselves in order to love others. And then, after the various approvals, came the result of the second part of the phrase: 'if however the grain dies it produces much fruit' (John 12 : 24).

In those years many branches were born from the one tree. In 1967 around the married focolarini thousands and thousands of families found new vigour, new relationships between partners, unity between parents and children, adoptions . . . the New Families were born. Around the volunteers, who want to animate the world of education, medicine, art and science and every expression of human life with the spirit of Christ (like the yeast in the dough) — the New Humanity Movement was born. Around the priests who have taken this spirit as their own — the Priests' Movement has grown, and many new vocations flourish. Those who are parish priests animate the life of their parishes so as to make this cell of the Church an ecclesial family in accordance with the living example of the early community in Jerusalem. All these parishes together form the New Parishes Movement. The past few years have seen our spirit deeply penetrating many religious congregations and orders of men and women. The fruits are: renewal of the community, rediscovery of the founder's charism, revaluation of the rules, and new members.

In these same years, the second generation of the Focolare Movement began taking shape — the Gen (New Generation). About 12,000 young boys and girls and young men and women who commit themselves in a total way make up the Gen units, and communicate their life to tens of thousands of other young people. Charged with the impetus of the Gospel, they go against the current in a world disturbed by protest, drugs, sex and juvenile crime. They promote the unity of all peoples and unity between generations. By the witness of their experience of living the Gospel, and through songs, mime and dance, they launch the message of the Gospel among young people in every continent, with exceptional results.

They work together all over the world in order to help the Focolarini to build a little town for the Bangwa tribe in the Cameroon, which I mentioned at the beginning. A hospital, schools, small industries, an electric generator have been built. They succeed: there at Fontem, 8,000 animists have requested baptism because they have seen the mutual love between whites and blacks. People from surrounding countries go there to see what the world would be like if everyone lived the Gospel. Like at Fontem, five other little towns have started. They resemble each other because all their inhabitants try to live the Gospel, and at the same time are different because they are suited to the needs of the various peoples. They are at O'Higgins, Argentina; at San Paolo and Recife in Brazil; at Loppiano, Italy, and Ottmaring, Federal Germany.

Movement Crossed Church Barriers

But the Movement not only crossed the political boundaries of more than one hundred countries, it has also gone beyond the barriers erected for centuries between the various Christian churches. This is how it happened. As usual we had no plan. Three German Lutheran pastors were present at a small speech I gave in a convent of the Marienschwestern, and their reaction was 'what? — are Catholics living the Gospel?' And they arranged at once with my friends to introduce this life to their brotherhoods, groups, and Lutheran parishes in Germany. Centuries old prejudices collapsed on both sides. The Lutherans understood many things. We admired in them their love of Scripture and their spirit of prayer. They wanted to deepen the new life which they wished to share with us at least in part. And they came to Rome almost every year for an ecumenical meeting. At a certain point, meetings were not enough, and we decided to start a centre for common life for members of the two denominations at Ottmaring, near Augsburg, precisely where in 1530 the division between Lutherans and Catholics was affirmed. The permission of the Catholic bishop was encouraging as was that of the Lutheran bishop. Around this centre the little town is developing which was already mentioned. And also other groups of Lutherans, Baptists, and members of the Free Church from the North and the South of Germany meet there together, who have adopted the spirit of the Focolare Movement, while remaining faithful to their churches.

Some Anglican clergy and laity were enthusiastic about this experience and they wished to bring it to the Church of England. In 1966, the then Archbishop of Canterbury, Dr. Ramsey, received me in an audience. He concluded by saying that he saw God's hand in this Movement and he invited me to bring this spirit to Anglican groups. Today the Focolare Movement is living and growing among Anglicans all over the United Kingdom.

In Switzerland the Movement is alive among many members of the Swiss Reformed Church. The words of Jesus which they too emphasize, 'Where two or three are gathered in my name, I am there among them' (Matthew 18 : 20), make them feel an affinity with us. We have also got to know the Prior of Taizé and established a friendship with him, and also with some of the various personalities of the World Council of Churches. In North America where the Movement has been since 1960, there are many Christians of different denominations who share our spirit. On June 13th, 1967, the Ecumenical Patriarch of Constantinople, Athenagoras I, was expecting me. He had heard something about us, but wanted to know more. It is impossible to describe how attached he was to the Movement. He emphasized love and life above all. I made several journeys in the next five years to Istanbul. My visits had the aim of keeping him informed, but above all of healing the deep wound of the incomplete unity with Rome. The circumstances were not yet ripe. Athenagoras was one of the greatest men of our age. Yet he wanted to be, as he put it, 'a simple member of this Movement'. Like a prophet he foretold: 'The day will come, the sun will rise high, the angels will sing and dance, and all of us, Bishops and Patriarchs, will be around the Pope celebrating with the one chalice.' It is through him that the Focolare Movement w as born and is spreading among the Orthodox, especially in the Near East.

Other Faiths

But in the world there are various religions. The wide expansion of the Movement brings us face to face with persons of other faiths. With the faithful of the noble and tortured Jewish people dialogue is easy. We share with them part of Revelation. We are grateful to them for having given us a Jewish Jesus, Jewish Apostles. And Mary too was Jewish.

In the Moslems we admire their tenacious love for religion. They are an example to us. The mystic of the Islamic tradition, Al-Hallaj, wrote: 'In His Essence (In the essence of God), Love is the essence of essences.'

In Asia we met Buddhists. It is good for our soul to remember the words of Buddah: 'Like a mother who even at risk to her own life watches and protects her only son, so with a great soul we must . . . love the whole world. . . .'

The words of the Indian mystic Ramakrishna strike us: 'Only love matters. Have love for everyone: nobody is any different from you. God lives in everyone and nothing exists without him.'

We are in contact with Hindus and also with Shintoists. The dialogue which the members of the Movement established with these brothers of other religions is not made up of words. We love them as they are, concerning ourselves about everything to do with them and therefore also about their religious life. Our love is returned and meetings are held which are often large, in which the concern of everyone is to seek together the truths which most unite us in order to live them together and to tell each other about the experiences which show our concern for God and our brothers, and this concern has spread more and more widely. The faithful of the great religions, when they come into contact with the Movement, sense that a new current of love runs through the world, and they like to call themselves, according to what they feel deep inside themselves: Moslem Gen, or Buddhist Volunteers or Gen, and so on.

But the mass of people who pain our heart are the atheists of east and west: they are the poorest people. The witness of our Christian unity over the years has struck many of them who have come back to God.

This is everything. Pope Paul VI, after having seen 25,000 of our young people gathered together in St. Peter's during Holy Year, said: 'A new world is born.' Yes, this is my experience: through our Movement and other movements of God, the world of love is coming to life without fuss. The future will be rich in surprises.

But I cannot conclude this talk without offering my deeply felt thanks to Mr. and Mrs. Templeton, who perhaps cannot imagine the marvellous results of their initiative. I also thank all those who have taken part in making this award. May God reward them.

The Use of the Money

I shall use the prize money to enlarge the maternity wing of the hospital in the little town of Fontem in the Cameroon; to build two houses for those who are living in the shanty town, the mocambos in Recife (Brazil), and to build the last stage of a religious and social training centre for Asians, at Tagaytay in the Philippines. I will keep a part of the prize for the 'Town of Charity' which the diocese of Rome is setting up for handicapped people.

As a memory of this day I would like to leave with you the words of the great Spanish mystic, John of the Cross: 'Where you do not find love, put love and you will find love.'

SELECTED BIBLIOGRAPHY

Chiara, an authorised biography by Edwin Robertson. Christian Journals Ltd., Belfast (1977).

FIRST BROCHURE ON THE TEMPLETON FOUNDATION PRIZE

Purpose

The Templeton Foundation Prize for Progress in Religion has been established to call attention to and provide recognition of ideas, insights, actions, accomplishments, etc., which have been or may be instrumental in widening or deepening man's knowledge and love of God, and thereby furthering the quest for the quality of life that mirrors the divine.

The Templeton Prize will be awarded, ordinarily on the annual schedule, to a living person who may be a representative of any religious tradition or movement. In nominations for the Prize there shall be no limitation of race, creed, sex or geograaphical background.

Objectives

The objective of the Templeton Prize is to stimulate the knowledge and love of God on the part of mankind everywhere. Such an attitude and such a relationship have their own intrinsic value. 'Man's chief end is to glorify God and to enjoy Him for ever.' Man was created by God for fellowship with Him, to know Him, and to worship and serve

Him. Man's heart remains restless until it finds rest in God. Progress is needed in religion as in all other dimensions of human experience and endeavour. There has been a long departure, at least in Western culture, from the last synthesis when religious knowledge and scientific knowledge were organically related. It is imperative that progress in religion be accelerated as progress in other disciplines takes place. A wider universe demands a deeper awareness of the dimension of the spirit and of its spiritual resources available for man, of the immensity of God, and of the divine knowledge and understanding still to be claimed.

The Templeton Prize serves to stimulate this quest for deeper understanding and pioneering breakthroughs in religious knowledge by calling attention annually to the achievements that are being made in this area. It is hoped that there will result from this enterprise a deeper spiritual awareness on the part of men, a better understanding of the meaning of life, a heightened quality of devotion and love, and a greater emphasis on the kind of dedication that brings the human life more into concert with the divine will, thus releasing new and creative energies into human society today.

Criteria for selection

The judges will consider a nominee's contribution to the knowledge and love of God made during the year prior to his selection or during his entire career. Qualities sought in awarding the Prize will be freshness, creativity, innovation and effectiveness. Such contribution may involve a study, or a life, or the inspiration of a new movement or thrust in religion, or a religious institution. Examples are pioneering and innovative study in the field of religious development of new forms of worship and devotion, fashioning of new and effective methods of communicating faith, creation of new schools of thought, creation of new structures of understanding the relationship of God to the universe, to the physical sciences, the life sciences, and the human or man sciences, the releasing of new and vital impulses into old religious structures and forms, etc.

Nominations

The Templeton Prize will be awarded on the decision of a panel of nine judges, who are representative of the major faiths of the world today. It is anticipated that the Prize will be given annually, although the panel of judges reserves the right to withold the Prize any given year when a worthy recipient has not been nominated.

Nominations will be sought from a wide constituency that will include all the major religions of the world. Official organizations will be invited to submit nominations, and leaders of theological and religious institutions will be contacted for nominations.

All nominations will be considered by a central committee, with finalists then being submitted to the panel of judges, whose decision will be final.

The award

The Prize, a sum in the amount of £34,000 sterling or its equivalent, will be awarded in December each year at the celebration in honour of the recipient held in London. It is anticipated that the first award will be made in 1973.

Judges

The Reverend Dr Eugene Carson Blake is General Secretary of the World Council of Churches which brings together 255 churches in some 90 countries. Prior to his present appointment in 1966 he was the chief executive officer of the United Presbyterian Church in the U.S.A. A widely travelled churchman, he has led a quest for a greater understanding of God in international affairs and for peace with justice in areas of conflict. Born in the U.S.A. in 1906 he has received numerous university and state awards since graduating from Princeton University in 1928.

Professor Suniti Kumar Chatterji, a Hindu, is the National

Professor of India in Humanities. Born in Sibpur Howrah, Bengal, in 1890 and educated in Calcutta, London and Paris, Porfessor Chatterji has held university posts in India and the U.S.A. He has received doctorates from several universities and the Order of the Republic of India. He is a member of the Norwegian Academy of Sciences and the cultural associations of several countries. Among his publications in the English, Bengali and Hindi languages are : *Language and Literature of Modern India*, *Origin and Development of the Bengali Language* and, more recently, *Africanism and the African Personality*, *Balts and Aryans in their Indo-European Background*, *India and Ethiopia from the 17th century B.C.* and *World Literature and Tagore* (1971). And listed among his leisure interests are the collecting of small art and listening to music.

Sir Muhammad Zafrulla Khan is President of the International Court of Justice at the Hague. He is a former judge of the Supreme Court of India (1941-47) and was Pakistan's Foreign Minister from 1947-54. In 1962 he was elected President of the 17th Session of the United Nations General Assembly. Born in 1893, he graduated with Honours in Arabic from the Government College, Lahore, and studied Law in Lincoln's Inn, London, where he was called to the Bar in 1914. He has received several University awards in England and the U.S.A., and in 1945 was made an Honorary Bencher of Lincoln's Inn, London. In 1926 he was elected a member of the Punjab Legislative Council and held the seat until 1935. From 1935-45 he was a member of the Viceroy's Cabinet (India). Sir Zafrulla Khan is a noted Islamic scholar and has published a number of books, including *Islam : Its Meaning for Modern Man* and *Islamic Worship*.

Dr Margaretha Klompé is a leading Roman Catholic in Holland and in 1956 was the first Dutch lady to become a cabinet minister. She was born in 1912, studied chemistry and physics at the University of Utrecht and was for many years a school-teacher. She was a member of the Consul-

134

tative Assembly of the Council of Europe and of the Coal and Steel Assembly, and several times delegate to the U.N., Minister of Social Welfare from 1956-63, and Minister of Cultural Affairs, Recreation and Social Welfare from 1966-71. Dr Klompé has been to the forefront in the search for a deeper understanding between the peoples of the world. She is a member of the Pontifical Commission on Justice and Peace of the Roman Catholic Church.

Sir Alan Mocatta is a judge of the Queen's Bench Division of the High Court in England and President of the Restrictive Practices Court. Sir Alan, who is 64, is President of the Congregation of Spanish and Portuguese Jews and a former Chairman of the Council of Jews' College. Born in 1907, he belongs to one of the oldest Anglo-Jewish families. The Mocattas first arrived in England in 1671. Sir Alan's communal activities started at the Oxford Synagogue where he officiated at the services and held the office of Warden. A strong sense of duty, a fresh and active mind and a balanced judgement have enabled him to produce solutions to the seemingly intractable problems. He is keenly interested in cricket and until four years ago was always happy to play for the local Cornish side where he escapes during the summer holidays. Nowadays he and his wife spend much of their vacations trout and salmon fishing.

Dr James McCord is President of Princeton Theological Seminary in New Jersey and a noted theologian throughout the world. He is the North American Secretary of the World Alliance of Reformed Churches and is Chairman of the Committee on the Consultation on Church Union of the United Presbyterian Church in the U.S.A. A member of the Commission of Faith and Order of the World Council and Chairman of the Department of Faith and Order of the National Council of Churches in the U.S.A., Dr McCord is also Chairman of the Commission on Accrediting of the American Association of Theological Schools. He is the editor of *Supplementa Calviniana* and other noted books. Born in Texas in 1919, Dr McCord was educated at Austin

College, New College, Edinburgh, and Harvard University. Abbot Kosho Ohtani, a Buddhist of the authoritative Nishi Hongwanji Temple, is the Patriarch of the Shin Sects, one of the principal denominations of Japanese Buddhism. He became Priest of the Nishi Hongwanji in 1927 and Patriarch in 1935. A graduate of Tokyo University, he has written several important books including *Buddhistic Ritual in Tao Era* and *The Meaning of Being Taught*. Born on November 1st, 1911, to Abbot Koymo Ohtani, he was adopted by Abbot Kozui Ohtani as his heir apparent. He is married to the elder daughter of Prince Tokudaiji.

The Right Reverend Robin Woods is the Anglican Bishop of Worcester in England. He is a former Dean of Windsor and Domestic Chaplain to the Queen. Born in 1914, Bishop Woods graduated from Cambridge and, from 1937 to 1942, was an assistant Secretary to the Student Christian Movement. He was an Army Chaplain during the Second World War and in 1951 was appointed Archdeacon of Singapore. Returning to England as Archdeacon of Sheffield he became deeply involved in the work of industrial missions. He was a joint Secretary of the talks on union between the Church of England and the Methodist Church and has played a constructive part in the ecumenical movement. Married, with a family of two boys and three girls, the bishop paints and plays the piano. He was awarded the Knight Commander of the Royal Victorian Order (K.C.V.O.) on leaving Windsor in 1971.

Lord Thurlow, who recently retired as Governor of the Bahamas, is a member of the Church of England and has long been interested in relations between the world religions. He has held diplomatic posts in Canada, Ghana, New Zealand and India, and was a member of the British delegation at the United Nations General Assemblies in 1946 and 1948, and at the Paris Peace Conference in 1946. Prior to his being appointed Governor of the Bahamas, Lord Thurlow was British High Commissioner in Nigeria.

Born in England on March 9th, 1912, he was educated at Shrewsbury School and Trinity College, Cambridge.

1972

TEMPORARY BROCHURE ON THE TEMPLETON FOUNDATION PRIZE

Purpose

The Templeton Foundation Prize for Progress in Religion was established to call attention to a variety of persons who have found new ways to increase man's love and understanding of God. It is aimed at providing recognition of ideas, insights, accomplishments which have been or may be instrumental in widening or deepening man's knowledge and love of God and thereby furthering the quest for the quality of life that mirrors the Divine.

The Templeton Prize is awarded annually to a living person who may be a representative of any religious tradition or movement. The Templeton Prize does not encourage syncretism but rather an understanding of the benefits of diversity. It seeks rather to focus attention on the wide variety of highlights in present-day religious thought and work. It does not seek a unity of denominations or a unity of world religions; but rather it seeks to encourage understanding of the benefits of diversity. There is no limitation of race, creed, sex or geographical background.

Objective

An objective of the Templeton Prize is to stimulate the knowledge and love of God on the part of mankind everywhere. Such an attitude and such a relationship have their own intrinsic value. 'Man's chief end is to glorify God and to enjoy Him forever.' Man was created by God for fellowship with Him, to know Him, and to worship and serve Him. Man's heart remains restless until it finds rest in God.

This is not a prize for religion. It is not a prize for saintliness or mere good and just works. It is a prize for progress. And progress is needed in religion as in all other dimensions of human experience and endeavour. There has been a long departure, at least in Western culture, from the last synthesis when religious knowledge and scientific knowledge were organically related. It is imperative that progress in religion be accelerated as progress in other disciplines takes place. A wider universe demands a fresh look at the dimension of the spirit and of the spiritual resources available to man, of the immensity of God, and of the divine knowledge and understanding still to be claimed.

The Templeton Prize serves to highlight original and fruitful spiritual projects : to act as a catalyst in the quest for deeper understanding and pioneering breakthroughs in religious knowledge. It is hoped that there will be the opening up of religious thought to a wider vision of God's infinity : a deeper spiritual awareness on the part of men, a better understanding of the meaning of life and a heightened quality of devotion and love, thus releasing new and creative energies into human society.

Criteria for selection

The judges consider a nominee's contribution to progress in religion made either during the year prior to his selection or during his entire career. The qualities sought in awarding the Prize are : freshness, creativity, innovation and effectiveness. Such contribution may involve a study or a life, new concepts of the spirit, new organizations, new methods of evangelism, new and effective ways of communicating God's wisdom and infinite love, creation of new schools of thought, creation of new structures of understanding the relationship of God to the universe, to the physical sciences, the life sciences, and the human or man sciences, the releasing of new and vital impulses into old religious structures and forms, etc.

Nominations

The Templeton Prize is awarded on the decision of a panel of nine judges, who are representative of the major faiths of the world today. The Prize is given annually, although the panel of judges reserves the right to withhold the Prize any given year when a worthy recipient has not been nominated.

Nominations are sought from a wide constituency that includes all the major religions of the world. Official organizations are invited to submit nominations and leaders of theological and religious institutions and those engaged in innovative and creative work are contacted for nominations. Other persons desiring to nominate should write to the Templeton Foundation, care of: The Reverend Wilbert Forker, 2 Bristow Park, Upper Malone Road, Belfast BT9, 6TH, Northern Ireland.

All nominations are considered by a central committee, with finalists then being submitted to the panel of judges, whose decision is final.

The Award

The Prize, a sum in the amount of £40,000 sterling or its equivalent, is awarded each year at a ceremony in honour of the recipient.

Judges

Her Majesty Fabiola, Queen of the Belgians, was born on the 11th June, 1928. She speaks French, Dutch, English and German fluently, as well as her mother tongue Spanish. From her youth her main concerns have been in cultural and social fields. She is interested in problems concerned with young people and in music, painting and poetry. On the 15th December, 1960, she married Baudouin, King of the Belgians. The Queen follows the country's cultural and artistic life very closely. She is deeply interested in the development of ethical and spiritual issues. She shares with the King a deep concern for all human problems, many aspects of which they have frequently encountered on their numerous tours, both in their own country and abroad.

His All Holiness Demetrios I is the 269th Archbishop of Constantinople, New Rome and Ecumenical Patriarch. He succeeded Patriarch Athenagoras I, who died in 1972. The Ecumenical Patriarch is the spiritual leader of 14 autocephalous Orthodox churches around the world with a total of 126 million members. The seat of the Patriarchate is the Phanar in Istanbul. The Patriarch was born Demetrios Papadopoulos in Istanbul in 1914, and educated in Greek- and French-speaking schools there. His theological studies were at the now-closed Patriarchal seminary on the island of Halki. In 1937 he became a deacon and worked in an Istanbul parish, held an assignment in Greece and became a priest in 1942. From 1945 to 1950 he was chaplain to the Greek community in Teheran and taught classical Greek at the university. Returning to Istanbul, he became Vicar General of Ferikoy, an Istanbul suburb, and was consecrated Bishop of Eleia. In February 1972 he was named Archbishop of Imbros and Tenedos, islands at the mouth of the Dardanelles. Six months later he was chosen Ecumenical Patriarch by the fifteen metropolitans of the Holy Synod.

Sir Muhammad Zafrulla Khan is a former President of the International Court of Justice at the Hague and a former Judge of the Supreme Court of India (1931-47). He was Pakistan's Foreign Minister from 1947-54. In 1972 he was elected President of the 17th Session of the United Nations General Assembly. Born in 1893, he graduated with Honours in Arabic from the Government College, Lahore, and studied Law in Lincoln's Inn, London, where he was called to the Bar in 1941. He has received several University awards in England and the U.S.A., and in 1945 was made an Honorary Bencher of Lincoln's Inn, London. In 1926 he was elected a member of the Punjab Legislative Council and held the seat until 1935. From 1935-45 he was a member of the Viceroy's Cabinet (India). Sir Zafrulla is a noted Islamic scholar and has published a number of books, including *Islam : Its Meaning for Modern Man* and *Islamic Worship*.

The Reverend Dr James McCord is President of Princeton Theological Seminary in New Jersey (U.S.A.) and a noted theologian throughout the world. He is the North American Secretary of the World Alliance of Reformed Churches and was the first Chairman of the Consultation on Church Union. A member of the Commission on Faith and Order of the World Council and the first Chairman of the Department of Faith and Order of the National Council of Churches in the U.S.A.; Dr McCord is also Chairman of the Commission on Accrediting of the American Association of Theological Schools. He is the editor of *Supplementa Calviniana* and other noted books. Born in 1919, Dr McCord was educated at Austin College, New College, Edinburgh, and Harvard University.

The Reverend Dr Norman Vincent Peale has been the minister of Marble Collegiate Reformed Church in New York City since 1932. He is well known in the United States and throughout the world as both a writer and a preacher. He is editor of the mass-circulation inspirational magazine *Guideposts*, though he is better known through his book *The Power of Positive Thinking*. Dr Peale is a Trustee of Ohio Wesleyan Union Central College; a member of the Executive Committee of the Presbyterian Ministers Fund for Life Insurance; and Mid-Century White

House Conference on Children and Youth; President of the National Temperance Society and the Protestant Council of the City of New York; and a lecturer on public affairs and personal effectiveness.

Her Serene Highness Princess Poon Pismai Diskul is a member of the Thai royal family and President of the World Fellowship of Buddhists. Her Serene Highness is also a Vice-President of the Buddhist Association of Thailand. The princess, who is a member of the Committee for the Revision of Thai History, is a leading Thai historian. She has been acknowledged for her devotion to the cause of world peace and for her efforts in the renaissance of Buddhism. She has recently visited Buddhist centres in Europe, U.S.A., Canada and the Far Eastern countries, delivering lectures on Buddhism.

Mr Edmund Leopold de Rothschild is President of the Bank of Rothschilds and Chairman of N. M. Rothschild & Sons Ltd. Born in London in 1916, Mr de Rothschild was educated at Harrow School and Trinity College Cambridge. Outside his full business life Mr de Rothschild takes a significant role in community affairs. His particular interest in Christian-Jewish dialogue has extended over many years through his involvement with the Council of Christians and Jews of which he is Treasurer in Great Britain. He was Joint Treasurer of the United Kingdom for World Refugee Year and Trustee appointed by the British Government for the Freedom from Hunger Campaign. Since 1967 he has travelled extensively seeing world leaders in an effort to relieve the plight of the refugees in the Middle East.

The Right Reverend Robin Woods is the Anglican Bishop of Worcester in England. He is a former Dean of Windsor and Domestic Chaplain to the Queen. Born in 1941, Bishop Woods graduated from Cambridge and from 1937-42, was an assistant Secretary to the Student Christian Movement. He was an Army Chaplain during the Second World War and in 1951 was appointed Archdeacon of Singapore. Returning to England as Archdeacon of Sheffield he became deeply involved in the work of industrial missions. He was a joint Secretary of the talks on union between the Church of England and the Methodist Church and has played a constructive part in the ecumenical movement. Married, with a family of two boys and three girls, the bishop paints and plays the piano. He was created a Knight Commander of the Royal Victorian Order (K.C.V.O.) in 1971.

A further appointment is to be announced later this year.

Former judges

The Reverend Dr Eugene Carson Blake who was General Secretary of the World Council of Churches.

Professor Suniti Kumar Chatterji, National Professor of India in the Humanities.

Dr Margaretha Klompé, the first Dutch lady to become a cabinet minister.

Sir Alan Mocatta who is a Judge of the Queen's Bench Division of the High Court in England and President of the Restrictive Practices Court.

The Lord Abbot Kosho Ohtani, Patriarch of Nishi Hongwanji Temple, Japan.

The Right Hon. Lord Thurlow, former Governor of the Bahamas.

Recipients

1973 Mother Teresa of Calcutta.
1974 Brother Roger, Prior of the Taizé Community in France.
1975 Dr Sarvepalli Radhakrishnan, former President of India.

May, 1975

appendix c

SECOND BROCHURE ON THE
TEMPLETON FOUNDATION PRIZE

Purpose

The Templeton Foundation Prize for Progress in Religion was established to call attention to a variety of persons who have found new ways to increase man's love of God or man's understanding of God. It seeks to help people of all nations to her about the rich variety of new spiritual concepts and organizations. Also to help people to see the infinity of the Universal Spirit still creating the galaxies and all living things and the variety of ways in which the Creator is revealing himself to different people. The programme is aimed at providing recognition of ideas, insights or accomplishments which have been or may be instrumental in widening or deepening man's knowledge or love of God and thereby furthering the quest for the quality of life that mirrors the Divine.

The Templeton Prize is awarded annually to a living person who may be a representative of any religious tradition or movement. The Templeton Prize does not encourage syncretism but rather an understanding of the benefits of diversity. It seeks rather to focus attention on the wide variety of highlights in present-day religious thought and work. It does not seek a unity of denominations or a unity of world religions; but rather it seeks to encourage understanding of the benefits of diversity. There is no limitation of race, creed, sex or geographical background.

Objectives

An objective of the Templeton Prize is to stimulate the knowledge and love of God on the part of mankind everywhere. Man is created by God for fellowship with Him, to know Him, and to worship and serve Him.

This is not a prize for religion. It is not a prize for saintliness nor mere good works nor social justice nor racial justice nor peace. It is a prize for progress. And progress is needed in religion as in all other dimensions of human experience and endeavour. It is imperative that progress in religion be accelerated as progress in science and other disciplines takes place. A wider universe demands a fresh look at the omnipresence of the spirit and of the spiritual resources available to man, of the immensity of God, and of the divine knowledge and understanding still to be claimed.

The Templeton Prize serves to highlight original and fruitful spiritual projects: to act as a catalyst in the quest for deeper understanding and pioneering breakthroughs in religious knowledge. It is hoped that there will be the opening up of religious thought to a wider vision of God's infinity: a deeper spiritual awareness on the part of men, a better understanding of the meaning of life and a heightened quality of devotion and love, thus releasing new and creative energies into human society.

Criteria

The judges consider a nominee's contribution to progress in religion made either during the year prior to his selection or during his entire career. The qualities sought in awarding the Prize are: freshness, creativity, innovation and effectiveness. Such contribution may involve a study or a life, new concepts of the spirit, new organizations, new methods of evangelism, new and effective ways of communicating God's wisdom and infinite love, creation of new schools of thought, creation of new structures of understanding the relationship of God to the universe, to the physical sciences, the life sciences, and the human or man sciences, the releasing of new and vital impulses into old religious structures and forms, etc.

Nominations

The Templeton Prize is awarded annually on the decision of a panel of nine judges, who are representative of the major faiths of the world today.

Nominations are sought from leaders of all the major religions of the world. Leaders of theological and religious institutions and those engaged in innovative and creative work are invited to submit nominations. Other persons desiring to nominate should write to the Templeton Foundation, care of: The Reverend Wilbert Forker, 2 Bristow Park, Upper Malone Road, Belfast BT9, 6TH, Northern Ireland.

All nominations are considered by a central committee, with finalists then being submitted to the panel of judges, whose decision is final.

Award

The Prize, a sum in the amount of £50,000 sterling or its equivalent, is awarded each year at a ceremony in honour of the recipient, at which the recipient delivers a lecture.

Judges

Her Majesty Fabiola, Queen of the Belgians, was born on the 11th June, 1928. She speaks French, Dutch, English and German fluently, as well as her mother tongue Spanish. From her youth her main concerns have been in cultural and social fields. She is interested in problems concerned with young people in music, painting and poetry. On the

15th December, 1960, she married Baudouin, King of the Belgians. The Queen follows the country's cultural and artistic life very closely. She is deeply interested in the development of ethical and spiritual issues. She shares with the King a deep concern for all human problems, many aspects of which they have frequently encountered on their numerous tours, both in their own country and abroad.

His All Holiness Demetrios I is the 269th Archbishop of Constantinople, New Rome and Ecumenical Patriarch. He succeeded Patriach Athenagoras I, who died in 1972. The Ecumenical Patriarch is the spiritual leader of fourteen autocephalous Orthodox churches around the world with a total of 126 million members. The seat of the Patriarchate is the Phanar in Istanbul. The Patriarch was born Demetrios Papalopoulos in Istanbul in 1914, and educated in Greek- and French-speaking schools there. His theological studies were at the now-closed Patriarchal seminary on the island of Halki. In 1937 he became a deacon and worked in an Istanbul parish, held an assignment in Greece and became a priest in 1942. From 1945-50 he was chaplain to the Greek community in Teheran and taught classical Greek at the university. Returning to Istanbul, he became Vicar General of Ferikoy, an Istanbul suburb, and was consecrated Bishop of Eleia. In February 1972 he was named Archbishop of Imbros and Tenedos, islands at the mouth of the Dardanelles. Six months later he was chosen Ecumenical Patriarch by the fifteen metropolitans of the Holy Synod.

Sir Bernard Lovell, Professor of Radio Astronomy of the University of Manchester and Director of the Jodrell Bank Experimental Station (now Nuffield Radio Astronomy Laboratories), was a member of the Aeronautical Research Council from 1955-58, and of the Science Research Council from 1965-70. He was President of the Royal Astronomical Society for the period from 1969-71 and is an Honorary Fellow of the Society of Engineers, a Foreign Member of the American Academy of Arts and Sciences, an Honorary Life Member of the New York Academy and an Honorary Member of the Royal Swedish Academy. He is the holder of honorary degrees from a number of universities as well as a number of international awards, and was President of the British Association for the Advancement of Science in 1975.

Mr Apasaheb Balasaheb Pant, the former Ambassador of India to Italy, was Education Minister and Prime Minister (1944-48) of Aundh State (India); a member of the All India Congress Committee (1938); and alternate delegate of India at the United Nations (1951-52). He was Commissioner for the Government of India in British East Africa (1948-54); Consul General for the Belgian Congo and Ruanda-Urundi (1948-54), and concurrently Commissioner for Central Africa and Nyasaland (1950-54). He served as an Officer on Special Duty with the Ministry of External Affairs (1954-55) and was Political Officer, Sikkim and Bhutan, with control over Indian missions in Tibet (1955-61). He was Ambassador of India to Indonesia (1961-64), Norway (1964-66) and the U.A.R. (1966-69). Before taking up his last post he was High Commissioner of India in London (1969-72). Among his many publications are *Tensions and Tolerance* (1965), *Agression and Violence : Ghandian Experiments to Fight Them* (1968), *Yoga* (1968) and *Surya Namashar* (1969). In 1954 he was awarded the Padma Shri.

The Reverend Dr Norman Vincent Peale has been minister of Marble Collegiate Reformed Church in New York City since 1932. He is well known in the United States and throughout the world as both a writer and a preacher. He is editor of the mass-circulation inspirational magazine *Guideposts,* though he is better known through his book *The Power of Positive Thinking.* Dr Peale is a Trustee of Ohio Wesleyan Union Central College; a member of the Executive Commission of the Presbyterian Ministers Fund for Life Insurance; and Mid-Century White House Conference on Children and Youth; President of the National Temperance Society and the Protestant Council of the City of New York; and a lecturer on public affairs and personal effectiveness.

Her Serene Highness Princess Poon Pismai Diskul is a member of the Thai royal family and President of the World Fellowship of Buddhists. Her Serene Highness is also a Vice-President of the Buddhist Association of Thailand. The princess, who is a member of the Committee for the Revision of Thai History, is a leading Thai historian. She has been acknowledged for her devotion to the cause of world peace and for her efforts in the renaissance of Buddhism. She has recently visited Buddhist centres in Europe, U.S.A., Canada and the Far Eastern countries, delivering lectures on Buddhism.

Mr Edmund Leopold de Rothschild is President of the Bank of Rothschilds and Chairman of N. K. Rothschild & Sons Ltd. Born in London in 1916, Mr de Rothschild was educated at Harrow School and Trinity College Cambridge. Outside his full business life Mr de Rothschild takes a significant role in community affairs. His particular interest in Christian-Jewish dialogue has extended over many years through his involvement with the Council of Christians and Jews of which he is Treasurer in Great Britain. He was Joint Treasurer of the United Kingdom for World Refugee Year and Trustee appointed by the British Government for the Freedom from Hunger Campaign. Since 1967 he has travelled extensively seeing world leaders in an effort to relieve the plight of the refugees in the Middle East.

The Right Reverend John V. Taylor has been Bishop of Winchester since January 1975. He was warden of Bishop Tucker College, Mukono (Uganda) from 1945-54, Research Worker with the International Missionary Council from 1955-59, until becoming Africa Secretary, and later General Secretary, at the Church Missionary Society. He has published a number of books, particularly on Christian mission in Africa. He is a leading figure in the ecumenical movement and is the Prelate of the Most Noble Order of the Garter.

Mr Masakazu Echigo, who graduated in Economics from Kobe University in Japan, is the third Buddhist to be appointed to the Templeton award during the past four years. He is a leading member of the Hongwanji demomination of Japanese Buddhism and a principal Japanese industrialist. Mr Echigo, who is Chairman of C Itoh & Co Ltd — a major Japanese trading house, is also Director of the International Chamber of Commerce and Vice-President of the Japan Foreign Trade Council. He is also Director of a number of Japanese companies and Austrian Honorary Consul General in Osaka. In May 1971 he was awarded the second class of the Order of the Rising Sun by the Emperor of Japan. He was a recipient of the Blue Ribbon Medal from the Emperor in 1963.

Former Judges

The Reverend Dr Eugene Carson Blake who was General Secretary of the World Council of Churches.

Professor Suniti Kumar Chatterji, National Professor of India in the Humanities and past President of the Senate of Bengal.

Sir Muhammad Zafrulla Khan, a former President of the International Court of Justice at the Hague.

Dr Margaretha Klompé, the first Dutch lady to become a cabinet minister.

The Reverend Dr James I. McCord, President of Princeton Theological Seminary, Princeton, New Jersey (U.S.A.).

Sir Alan Mocatta who is a judge of the Queen's Bench Division of the High Court in England and President of the Restrictive Practices Court.

The Lord Abbot Kosho Ohtani, Patriach of the Nishi Hong-wanji Temple (Japan).

The Right Hon. The Lord Thurlow, former Governor of the Bahamas.

The Right Reverend R. W. Woods, Bishop of Worcester (England).

Recipients

1973   Mother Teresa of Calcutta, founder of the Missionaries of Charity.

1974   Brother Roger, Founder and Prior of the Taizé Community.

1975   Dr Sarvepalli Radhakrishnan, former President of India and Oxford Professor of Eastern Religions and Ethics.

1976   H.E. Léon Joseph Cardinal Suenens, Archbishop of Malines-Brussels.

August 1976